# Barbara Jean's
# Household
# Money Tips

## BARBARA GRUBER

E. P. DUTTON, INC.   New York

Published in the United States by E. P. Dutton, Inc., 2 Park Avenue, New
York, N.Y. 10016

Library of Congress Catalog Card Number: 83-70065

Published simultaneously in Canada by Clarke, Irwin & Company
Limited, Toronto and Vancouver

ISBN: 0-525-93294-1
10 9 8 7 6 5 4 3 2 1

First Edition

# CONTENTS

# INTRODUCTION

This book is intended to help you get more for your money. You will learn hundreds of tips to use every day. You do not have to go on a penny-pincher's budget. Instead, you will learn how to maximize your dollars by spending the smart way. Money is for the necessities and pleasures life has to offer. Implement my practical tips, and you can make your money go further.

Have a pen or pencil in your hand as you read. Star or underline the ideas that make sense to you. As you read, ideas will pop into your head. Jot them down in the book so you don't forget a single money-saving tip.

I want to help you get the most value for every dollar you spend.

*Barbara Jean*

# 1

# SMART SUPERMARKET SHOPPING

Most Americans spend thousands of dollars each year at the supermarket. Weekly grocery bills of $75 add up to almost $4,000 in a year's time. By spending just $10 less each week, you can save over $500 in one year. Follow my savvy shopping tips so you can start cutting your grocery bills immediately.

# YOU AND THE SUPERMARKET

You spend more time and more money in supermarkets than any other kind of store! That's why you need to know where and when to shop and how to see through merchandising gimmicks. Here is the help you need to make smart selections in the supermarket.

## Finding the best store

- Find out which store in your area has the best regular shelf prices. Here's how to do it: Make a list of about twenty items you buy regularly. Go to several stores, and jot down the cost of the items on your list in each store. To get an accurate price comparison, make certain to compare the exact same brand and quantity from store to store. That done, it should be easy to determine which one has the best regular shelf prices. Then shop there once a week only. Fewer trips to the store mean less spending.
- If you buy large quantities of a certain product, such as pet food, baby food, special diet items, double check to see which store has the best price on those items.
- Driving from store to store to buy advertised specials will save you money:

   if stores are conveniently located (the cost of driving your car can wipe out savings).
   if prices of specials are substantially lower than nonspecials.
   if you are buying items you would normally buy anyway (obviously, when you buy items you would not ordinarily buy, you are *not* saving money).

## Shopping

As a working mother, I do not have the time or inclination for multistop, marathon shopping trips. Instead, I've figured out which store in my area has the best shelf prices, and I shop there weekly. On my way home, I stop at one other supermarket to buy items on special (mostly produce and meat). Their regular shelf prices are very high, but their advertised items are worth a quick stop. I dash through the store, buying only the specials I've jotted down on my list, and then continue my trip homeward. If I went to that second supermarket on a separate trip, chances are that I'd buy some extra items. The best time to stop at another store for specials is on your way home from your big weekly shopping trip. That way you will spend less.

- **Shop when the stores are uncrowded.** When a store is a mass of carts, you may be tempted to buy things that don't make financial sense just to get out of the crowd. The best days to shop are Mondays through Thursdays. If you must shop on the weekend, get there first thing in the morning, when the store opens. Stores are most crowded on Friday nights and weekends—avoid these peak times if you possibly can.

- **Shop only once a week.** The fewer trips you make to the store, the less money you will spend. Dropping in at the supermarket for "just a few things" can result in a $20 bag of groceries. Instead, if you find you've run out of an item in midweek, change your meal plans, substitute or omit an ingredient, or borrow from a neighbor.

  If you must have an item or two, send one of your children to the store. It might be cheaper in the long run to have your child dash to a convenience store to buy one item at slightly higher prices, than for you to enter the store and wind up with a bagful of stuff.

- **Make a master grocery list of the items you customarily buy.** Follow your usual route through the store, jotting down items stocked in aisle 1, then aisle 2, and so on. Then the items on your master list will be in the order you come across them in the store. Have a number of photocopies made of this list, and every week post one on the refrigerator door (or other highly visible spot), circling items as you run out of them. Encourage family members to add items to the list, as they notice supplies running low. Then your list will be all compiled when you are ready to shop.

- **Cluster errands to save time and money.** Go to the supermarket, dry cleaner, and hardware store in one multishop trip. To keep meltables cold while you run other errands, take along your picnic ice chest, supplied with a block of ice, and store "must stay cold" items in it. Keep a supply of ice on hand by filling empty quart or half-gallon milk cartons with water and popping them in your freezer. (When I go shopping in warm weather, I also carry ice tea or juice in a travel mug, so I can have a cool drink in the midst of a hot shopping trip.)

- **Buy meats on special and save.** Meat is usually a high-ticket item, so stock your freezer when pork chops, ground beef, and roasts are at bargain prices. The amount you will want to keep on hand depends on the size of your family and the size of your freezer. Check pages 23–25 for some good ideas on getting the most from your freezer.

- **Get a rain check.** When the store has run out of items advertised on special, don't be afraid to request a rain check. Unless the ad states "while supplies last" or "limited quantity," grocers are supposed to maintain sufficient quantities of these products. If the checkout clerk suggests instead that you stop back the next day, point out that it takes time and gasoline to make a second trip and you prefer a rain check you can use the following week.

# Check out professional supply stores

Buying in quantity can save you money, especially on products that you use heavily, if you have room to store large containers. Check the Yellow Pages for businesses that supply shops or professional users of such products.

- Beauty-supply stores sell to the public as well as to beauticians. You won't get a professional discount from them, but you can still save money and get high-quality products. Buy shampoo and conditioner in gallon-size jugs and simply transfer the contents as needed into empty dishwashing-detergent containers. The large openings on shampoo bottles make you pour out more than you need and thus cause you to use up shampoo at a faster rate. You will be pleasantly surprised at how much less shampoo and conditioner you use when you keep them in containers with small openings. To avoid confusion, label the containers with a permanent marking pen. You can also buy combs, scissors, hair brushes and permanents at these stores at bargain prices.

- Feed stores sell pet foods in large quantities. You can buy everything from bird seed to dog biscuits. Dump the fifty-pound bag into a plastic garbage can with a tight-fitting lid. You can store the container in your garage or basement, and it will be safe from moisture and critters. If your kiddies give Rover a biscuit every time he walks in the room, buy biscuits in the smallest biscuit size available. A container of seventy small biscuits will last a lot longer than a box of twenty-four big ones.

Make friends with the green grocer in your market's produce section, and get free veggie trimmings for your hungry hamster. Ask your vet to recommend the most healthful diet for your pet—it may be cheaper than what you're feeding him now. For our dog, the vet suggested kibble mixed with table scraps and advised us to stay away from costly canned dog foods that are high in salt and fat.

## Guerrilla tactics

Buy, buy, buy—that's the merchandiser's message. The average supermarket contains over nine thousand items, whose producers use the most sophisticated of merchandising tricks to induce you to buy them—and at the highest possible price per ounce. Understanding these selling strategies will help you spend your food money the smart way and get the most nutrition for every dollar. To combat sales gimmicks, here are some points to think about.

**Spend it** tells you how you may be manipulated into paying too much for an item.

**Save it** gives you a smart-shopping strategy for outwitting the technique.

- Don't pay for packaging.

    **Spend it.** When selling rice, combine it with bouillon powder and dried herbs (a few pennies' worth of flavoring ingredients) and display the results on the box in full color, as part of a scrumptious meal. Quadruple the price.

    **Save it.** Ask yourself what you are really getting in that box. Does the price warrant the purchase? My rule of thumb is, the prettier the packaging, the *less* value for your money.

- Don't buy air space.

  **Spend it.** Keep the size of the box the same but put less inside. Change the indication of content weight on the box, to reflect the smaller amount (the law requires you to anyway), but the customer will never notice.

  **Save it.** Recheck price per ounce from time to time to make sure you are selecting the best buy. If the box feels lighter or appears to be less full, contents have probably been reduced.

- Watch out for Shrink-a-box.

  **Spend it.** Reduce the size of the package but keep the shape, color, and design the same—and the cost. The new Shrink-a-box will hold an ounce or two less, but the customer, if she notices the difference, will think she needs to visit her optometrist.

  **Save it.** If the box looks smaller, it probably is smaller. Recheck the cost per ounce to get the best buy.

- Combat Math Anxiety.

  **Spend it.** Package products in odd weights (9 pounds 3 ounces) to make computation difficult for consumers. It is hard to compare prices per ounce when boxes are odd weights.

  **Save it.** Bring your calculator to the supermarket and compute the cost per ounce. Find out how to compute cost per ounce on page 16.

- Wow—48 servings! Take a second look.

  **Spend it.** Make the customer think she is getting a lot for her money by stating the maximum number of servings imaginable.

  **Save it.** Figure out how much food you are getting and how many people in *your* family it will serve. The boxed macaroni-and-cheese dinner states that it contains four "standard servings." Actually, it could serve six toddlers or one teenager or two adults. What is a standard serving? My teenagers consider a standard serving of spaghetti to be three platefuls.

- Here comes Mr. Wonderful! Don't be fooled.

  **Spend it.** Show a gorgeous model dressed in red chiffon drinking flavored coffee with Mr. Wonderful. He watches adoringly while she stirs his wonder brew.

**Save it.** Don't let Madison Avenue clobber you with "image ads." If I buy that brand of flavored coffee mix, will handsome men come to drink it with me? I doubt it. Image ads sell you a high-priced product and a glimpse at a new way of life. What you really end up with is the high-priced product, period. The less nutritional foods are habitually the ones with the glamour ads. Think about it. Have you ever seen a full-color image ad for a ten pound sack of potatoes?

- Don't let the kids do all the choosing.

**Spend it.** Advertise products with child-appeal frequently during children's programs on television. Show the package often so nonreaders can instantly point it out to Mommy.

**Save it.** Swap babysitting with a friend or neighbor so you can shop without the children. If you must take the children with you to the supermarket, tie a toy or two to the shopping cart so they can play with it while sitting in the cart. Give older children the job of putting items *you* select into the grocery cart. If you do shop with children, tell them they get to pick just one item each week. If you shop with several children, let them take turns choosing an item on a weekly basis. If they are trying a new brand of cereal, buy the smallest box available even though it isn't the best buy per ounce. Then if the kids say "yuk!", you're not stuck with a monster-size box of Gorilla Granola.

- Resist high-priced add-ons and impulse items.

**Spend it.** Put bottles of expensive salad dressing and plastic salad tongs by the lettuce. Customers will be tempted to buy those items along with the produce. No price comparisons are possible because other brands of salad dressing are located elsewhere.

**Save it.** Resist the impulse to pick up an item you cannot price-compare.

- Take hype with a pinch of salt.

**Spend it.** Put signs on merchandise to attract the customer's attention. Use words like "Bargain Hunter's Delight," "Super-saver," "Solid Gold Value" . . .

**Save it.** Buyer, beware! When I compared prices on one so-called Supersaver Special Sale, I found that the sale items were priced *higher* than in other stores. It is up to you to know prices, check quantities and cost to get the best buy.

- Avoid being led into temptation.
  **Spend it.** Locate the dairy case at the farthest back wall of the market so that customers, making the long trek to pick up a quart of milk, will be exposed to several hundred products en route. Chances are that they will grab a few extra items.
  **Save it.** Avoid extra trips to the store. When you must make one, buy only what you came for.
- Compute price per ounce to be sure what you're paying.
  **Spend it.** Customers assume that they save money by buying the largest box of something, so stores often price the giant-size box at little or no saving. Few customers will actually verify the price. In fact, some stores even add a "point of purchase" sign to catch the customer's eye ("Inflation-Fighter Size").
  **Save it.** Compute the price per ounce to make sure you are getting the most for your money.

  Remember to keep these merchandising tactics in mind when you shop. The shopper who is alert to such gimmicks can easily avoid unnecessary spending. It's fun to keep an eye out for new grocers' tricks and to know you are too smart to fall for them.

# Second time around

- Since you pay for packaging, recycle it into something useful whenever possible.

| OLD CONTAINERS | NEW USE |
| --- | --- |
| wide-mouth jars | sprout seeds (page 21) |
| plastic detergent bottles | transfer shampoo/conditioner from giant jugs |
| plastic lids from coffee cans | snap one on bottom of the coffee can you are using so it does not scratch your counter top; put one on vegetable shortening can, too. |
| | coasters for plants |

| | |
|---|---|
| foam-plastic egg cartons | use to sprout seeds |
| empty milk cartons | rinse, fill with water, freeze for block ice. |
| foam-plastic meat trays | use for freezing foods (page 22) |
| ½ gallon juice or water bottles | use as container for frozen juice concentrate |
| plastic bleach jug | make a holder with a handle |
| | cut plastic into strips for plant markers and garden markers |

• Buy returnable containers whenever possible, because they cost less and result in less trash for you and the planet. And remember to return bottles to the store for deposits.

## Coupons

Are coupons real money savers? Yes, if you use them cleverly. Do *not* be tempted to buy high-priced convenience foods just because you see a coupon. Be aware that manufacturers use colorful and appealing coupon advertisements to create a demand for a product. But there's also no question that a selective use of coupons can be a terrific budget extender. So start building a practical collection of coupons today and see if you don't save.

• Clip coupons continually.   Check through your newspaper food section, Sunday supplements, and other sources of coupons (women's magazines, mailings, etc.) on a regular basis and clip those that interest you. Circle the expiration date to make sure you use them on time. And stash them in a handy file.

• Sort by category. If you keep a drawerful of coupons in one gigantic jumble, you won't be able to find the ones you need when you want them. So, store your coupons by category: canned/frozen foods; beverages; meats; household supplies; drug items; baking supplies; cereals; odds and ends; or whatever suits you. Clip coupons together or fasten with a rubber band, or keep them in clearly marked envelopes—use old envelopes that come with junk mail rather than buy new ones.

- Star items on your shopping list when you have a coupon. After you've drawn up your weekly list, go through your coupon file to find useful ones. Either staple these to the list, or mark those items with a star or "C". If you're in a hurry, simply take along the envelope.
- Start a coupon swap group with friends and neighbors to trade coupons you can't or don't use for those that you do. For example, a new mother would be eager for diaper and other baby-product coupons that a single person or older married wouldn't want. The same for pet owners and nonpet owners.
- Double-value days for coupons are worthwhile if they do not make you visit the store too often. Remember, extra trips to the store cost money, both in driving expenses and in those few extra items you may pick up while you're in the store. Supermarket managers deliberately invented double-coupon days to encourage customers to make special trips. Be alert to what you save and what you spend to assure that these days really pay off for you.

# New product madness

Totally useless items are sprinkled throughout every store. However, they must sell, or they would not be there. Products that do not generate sufficient dollars for the shelf space they occupy are quickly discontinued. Consequently strong competition exists among new products for the available shelf space, and that is why manufacturers often offer coupons for a new product they are introducing. Be alert to tempting but silly waste-of-the-money items you can live without in your grocery store.

- Double-face shelf-liner tape. Huh? I seem to have survived twenty years of homemaking without this goody. Maybe that's because I stopped lining cupboard shelves entirely when I found out there was a life beyond housework. This "wonderful" product holds shelf-lining paper in place in your cupboards. A better idea, which would save money, time, and work, would be *not* lining shelves with paper in the first place. Or, line them instead with vinyl adhesive paper that lasts virtually forever. If you are lucky enough to get hold of some linoleum scraps or wallpaper leftovers, they both serve as excellent lining for shelves.

- Toilet-bowl freshener. I confess, the water in our toilets is color-less—not sea green or Pacific blue. I'd rather spend my money on nutrition.
- Spray-on (aerosol, of course) flour and oil for baking pans. Imag-ine—for $1.59 I can grease and flour my baking pans with no mess, no taste, and a cleaner way for easier baking! I think I'll keep the $1.59 and just keep greasing and flouring pans the messy, old-fashioned way.
- Special cleaning compounds for tile, toilets, walls. Read the labels of the cleaning products in your cupboards. You may have some cleaning products that can be used for many purposes. Perhaps you can stop buying special products for certain cleaning jobs and use an all-purpose product instead.

# Resist temptation

Do you know who the smartest shoppers are? Sophisticated people in higher income brackets tend to be the most careful, best-informed spenders, while less-informed people who have the smallest amount of money tend to buy high-priced heavily merchandised foods. There's nothing tacky about seeing through all those Madison Avenue tactics and selecting the best buy for your money. So, be smart.

- Map your route. Research on "what makes people spend the most money" shows that the amount you spend in the supermarket depends on the *distance* you cover in the store. The more aisles you travel, up and down, the more merchandise you see and often buy. So, plan your trip to the supermarket as carefully as you plan a travel vacation.
- Set a cash limit. Don't take your checkbook to the supermarket. Take a certain amount of money, as much as you plan to spend on groceries. Do not carry extra cash along. When you know you only have a certain sum with you, you will be very price conscious. When you carry your checkbook and spend more than you planned, you simply write out a check for the cost of the food. When you use

the fixed-amount system, you have to put back items if you go over your limit. You might want to keep track of purchases with a calculator or clicker device as you go through the store.

- Stick to your list. Lists help you curb impulse buying. Make them out carefully, then stick to them.
- While you wait in the checkout line, here are some things to do:
    1. Reevaluate your purchases. Pick out anything you decide you don't want and give it to the grocery checker.
    2. Look through your coupons and gather up ones you can cash in toward purchases.
    3. Listen as the checker calls out prices. Question any price that does not seem right to you.
    Here are some things to *avoid* doing:
    1. Avoid buying candy and gum located at the check stand.
    2. Pass by maps, key chains, cigarette lighters, and junky magazines. These items are jammed into that area because managers know there is a captive audience of people in that line.

## SAVVY SHOPPING

Decisions, decisions, decisions! The average supermarket carries a mind-boggling array of over nine-thousand products! Become a savvy shopper and you'll wheel your way through the market making the "smartest picks" from the supermarket shelves.

# Choosing wisely

- Are store brands or name brands a better value? It depends on your private likes and dislikes and the quality of local products. In my supermarket, some store brands seem to be the same in taste, quality, and quantity as the famous brands, so I save money by purchasing them. I buy 24 ounces of store-brand lemon juice for 96¢ instead of the same quality in the brand advertised for $1.31. However, the store-brand canned tomatoes are *not* as good as the name brand I prefer, since the can contains more juice and fewer tomatoes. The container is cheaper, but you get less for your money. You will have to try store brands and name brands and compare them with one another. The same goes for generic no-brand items. Many are terrific. Give them a try to see which ones you like.

- Buy by the case if you can get it at a bargain price. Ask the store manager if he gives case discounts. If this is too much for you to use or store, perhaps you can split a case with a friend. The best choices for buying by the case are, of course, items that you use with great frequency anyway.

- Match form to function. In the main, large-size olives and whole nut meats are more expensive than the smaller sizes or broken nutmeats. So, if you are serving these items as appetizers, or using them to garnish a special dish, buy the more costly jumbo size. But whenever you plan to chop them up, use the less expensive varieties.

- Fresh food is usually a better buy, but not always so. It depends on the item you are purchasing. Canned sliced mushrooms cost almost $1 for a 4-ounce can. For the same price you can usually buy eight ounces of fresh mushrooms. So you get twice as many for the price, and fresh are more healthful because they are not packed in salt water. However, it is *not* cheaper to make fresh orange juice instead of using orange-juice concentrate. The frozen concentrate gives you more juice than you could make from fresh oranges that cost the same. Here's my secret for making frozen juice taste like fresh-squeezed: squeeze one or two fresh oranges and add that juice and pulp to the frozen juice. It makes an entire pitcherful taste fresh.

- Buy merchandise that is in good condition. Make certain that packages are not cut or torn open, cans are not dented, and jars and cans are not sticky. A damaged container may mean that the contents have been contaminated. If the only remaining cans of an item you want are dented, ask the manager to restock the shelves. If the item was on sale, get a rain check to use on your next trip to the store.

# Buy jumbo-size packages whenever possible

- Buying products in the largest-size boxes can cut down considerably on the price per ounce. However, compute the unit price first, to make sure it really is the best buy. Many consumers assume that the big box always saves them money, and manufacturers sometimes take advantage of this assumption. It's not always true, so check it out.
- Jumbo-size packages can be inconvenient to use at home. If the box of detergent is too heavy to lift, dump some of the contents into a plastic pail or dishpan and refill from the big box as needed.
- Don't buy the giant-size box of Crackle Crunchies if only one person likes them and they will get stale before you finish them. For perishable items, it is generally best to buy the size that your family consumes within a few days.

# Compare prices of different sizes

Be a price checker—it's easy if you do it my way.

- Don't bother checking every price every week. It is just too time-consuming. Instead, do it the quickie way. Next time you shop, check prices on each item you buy in aisles 1 and 2 in your market. The following week, check aisles 3 and 4, and so on. Each week concentrate on a different aisle or two in the store. It only takes a few moments, and it certainly pays. When you have gone through the entire store, start over again at aisle 1.
- How to do a quickie price check. Which item is the better buy?

|  |  |
|---|---|
| 24 ounces oil | 1 gallon oil |
| $1.35 | $5.86 |

First, you must figure out how much you are paying per ounce in each container. There are 32 ounces in a quart and 4 quarts in a gallon; $4 \times 32 = 128$ ounces in the gallon.

Tap 1.35 into your pocket calculator and divide by 24. This gives you the price per ounce for the small container.

Now tap 5.86 and divide by 128 to get the price per ounce of the large container.

$1.35 ÷ 24 = .056 per ounce      $5.86 ÷ 128 = .045 per ounce

In this case, the large jug of oil is the better buy.

- Manufacturers use odd weights to make it harder for you to calculate which is the better buy. With your trusty calculator it is not difficult. Change the fraction to a decimal. If the weight is 2¼, tap 2.25 into your calculator. Some packages have the weight in grams. Which is the better buy?

        60 gram can paprika      37 gram can paprika
        $1.03                   69¢

$1.03 ÷ 60 = .017 per gram
.69 ÷ 37 = .018 per gram

You pay less per gram in the larger can.

## Reach for a bargain

Get in the habit of looking at the shelves with care, top to bottom, back as well as front.

- Eye-level merchandise sells best, so that's where the grocer stores his high-priced markup items. If you see an 8-ounce box of seasoned rice mix for 68¢ on the eye-level shelf, drop your eyes to the bottom one. You may find a 28-ounce bag of plain rice for 73¢. The cheaper item, carrying smaller profit for the grocer, is placed where customers have to bend to get it. Get in the habit of looking for items bottom shelf first.
- Cans or packages in the back of the shelf may not be priced as high as those in front. My favorite salesclerk tells me that one of his least favorite jobs is changing prices on already shelved items. Often clerks will stamp all the easy-to-reach cans in the front of the shelf and ignore those behind. So, when you notice a price increase in one of your regular purchases, reach toward the back to see if there are containers that still carry the old price.

# Easy on the cook and the pocketbook

- Save both time and money by concentrating on quick-to-prepare, low-cost dishes. You can find all sorts of terrific recipes in ethnic cookbooks, time-saver cookbooks, and magazine articles for dishes that offer sound nutrition but don't cost a king's ransom.
- Find low-cost substitutes for exotic high-priced ingredients. If a recipe calls for pimientos, but a tiny jar costs a small fortune, simply use a red pepper or even a green pepper instead. If a friend tells you about a party dish that uses imported mushrooms, substitute a few domestic ones instead. Try chopped black olives in a recipe for caviar spread.
- Do you need a small amount of an unusual spice for a new recipe? Before buying a whole jar of your own, ask friends and neighbors if they have the spice on hand and if they will lend you a pinch. That way, you can experiment with unusual recipes without a major investment. I still have an almost untouched $3 jar of cardamom I bought to try a recipe my family didn't like.
- Eliminate expensive and time-consuming standbys. Many party recipes that I used to prepare are now prohibitively expensive, so I've weeded those out of my recipe file and at the same time chucked out all recipes that begin "start early in the day." There are many yummy dishes that do not cost the world and don't take all day to prepare.
- Ask your friends to share any low-cost recipes they love. This is my favorite way to get great new recipes.

# Switch to healthier snack foods

Most prepared snack foods (potato chips, corn chips, and so on) are high-priced and low in food value. Why not replace them with good-for-you, affordable foods, such as whole-grain crackers or muffins, celery stuffed with peanut butter, cored apples stuffed with crunchy peanut butter? Also, check out natural foods cookbooks and magazine articles for additional recipes and ideas.

Home-popped popcorn is always a great favorite and it's good for you. An electric corn popper makes the whole process easy and efficient, but any saucepan with a tight-fitting lid will do. To vary the flavor, sprinkle the popped corn with finely grated cheese, or seasoned salt.

Switch to nutritious, easy-on-the-budget cold drinks. Most children will drink canned soda all day long if you keep a supply on hand. This can get very expensive—and what's more, the drinks have no nutritive value. Instead, serve fruit juices and home-blended punches (two favorites are pink lemonade that gets its rich pink color from cranberry juice and a luscious three-fruit punch made from grape juice, orange juice and lemonade.) These are not only nutritious, they're easy on your budget as well. Keep a light-weight pitcher of juice or punch in the refrigerator, so the kids can help themselves. Or better yet, if you have a large picnic jug with a spout or spigot, fill it with juice and ice and keep it on the counter top in your kitchen.

## Common sense shopping

Avoid costly "diet" foods. Specialty items are always high priced, and low-calorie "diet" items cost a great deal more than standard brands while containing just slightly fewer calories. A fresh apple is a better buy than "diet" applesauce.

Natural juice is not the same as pure juice. Words like "organic," "health food," "natural" can mean many things. For $1.77, you can buy a half-gallon of orange juice that is 100 percent juice. Beside it in the dairy case is an orange drink that sells for $1.75 for the same quantity. There are pictures of oranges on the carton and the words "100 percent natural" pop out at you. But in small print it says, "60 percent juice." For 2¢ more, you can get 100 percent natural juice, not 60 percent juice and 40 percent water.

When you buy a product in an aerosol can, you pay for the aerosol. Many manufacturers now offer customers a choice between aerosol and nonaerosol versions of their products. For example, you can buy prewash solution in a 12-ounce can for $1.75, and for just 5¢

more you can get 22 ounces in the hand-pump version of the san brand. Also, aerosol cans often malfunction, so that you don't get the product that you pay for.

- Try cloth towels in place of paper. I stopped buying paper towe about three years ago when I started noticing how fast my fami used them up. As a substitute, I put up a hook near the sink a hung a hand towel from it. To drain bacon or other foods, I simp use a paper napkin. Spills can be wiped up with a sponge or clot With the high price of paper products, this has meant a big savin

- One nonfood item that used to chase up my grocery bill w charcoal for the barbecue. (We do a lot of outdoor entertaining, this was a big-ticket item for us.) It seemed that I was alway buying another bag of briquettes and another $2 can of lighting flui Now I buy about half as much charcoal, and I never buy lightir fluid. We purchased a kettle-type barbecuer that has a tight-fittir lid and vents that can be closed. When we finish cooking, we clos the vents and put the lid on, and the coals go out. Then we reus them for our next barbecue. For $5 we bought an electric start coil, safer and cheaper than flammable fluid and lasting for year After using, we unplug the sizzling hot coil and place it in an emp metal bucket or empty flower pot to cool.

- Cut your food bills by planting a vegetable garden. Vegetables c be grown in small areas and in containers. Find out which veget bles are most easily grown in your area by reading the garde section of the newspaper and checking with local gardeners an nurserymen. Gardening enthusiasts are usually delighted to shar their secrets of success.

- Incorporate some fruit trees into your landscaping. Our yard small, so we planted semi-dwarf trees. They take less room an yield a smaller crop. If you do get a large harvest all at onc consider doing some crop-swapping with friends and neighbors. W trade apples for nectarines with our neighbors every summer. Se page 24 for an idea for freezing extra fruit for use in pies.

- Once you've decided which crops to grow and chosen a spot fo your plot, buy the healthiest seedlings you can find. Most beginnin gardeners have greater success with seedlings, so they're a bette buy for novices than seeds.

After you've had some gardening experience, you'll probably want to grow your veggies from seed. Always buy seeds from a reliable source. Ask for suggestions from a gardening friend.

Share plants and tools with a neighbor. When you buy a six-pack of zucchini seedlings or tomato plants, keep three and trade three for other vegetables. You'll find that three flourishing tomato and zucchini plants will keep most people well supplied.

Grow your own sprouts for inexpensive, crunchy additions to salads and sandwiches. Use a wide-mouth jar, a rubberband, and a small clean piece of nylon stocking or cheesecloth. Buy seeds for sprouting in grocery stores or health food stores. For alfalfa sprouts, put 2 tablespoons of seeds in a jar and cover with a small amount of water. Soak overnight. Cap the jar with cheesecloth, held in place by the rubberband. Twice daily for a few days, drain water and then rinse seeds. Store the jar out of direct sunlight. (I keep my jar on the counter top in the kitchen so I don't forget to rinse the sprouts.) Before you know it, you will have a jarful of sprouts. Once they appear, transfer the jar to a sunny spot for a few hours and watch them turn green. Refrigerate and use. Sprouts are much cheaper to use when lettuce is out-of-season and priced sky high.

# MEALS FOR SAVINGS AND GOOD EATING

Saving money is a snap when you make the most of leftovers, use your freezer to maximum advantage and whip up your own convenience foods. Enlist the help of all family members in food preparation and clean-up.

## Leftovers and snacks

- If you have a microwave oven, put away leftovers in ready-to-eat portions on dishes that can be used for reheating in the microwave. Saves time and dirty dishes, and makes leftovers quick to use.
- Pick one location in the refrigerator where you always store

leftovers. Then you'll be sure to use them instead of having them get pushed to the back and forgotten. The same for snacks. I use foam-plastic tray and try to keep it filled with munchies. Some snac ideas:

> bagful of carrot sticks
> celery sticks
> cheese cubes (bite size)
> celery stalk filled with peanut butter or cream cheese
> cold cooked artichokes
> fruit
> bran muffins

- Leftovers can be saved up. Package, mark, and freeze a leftove dish in one-person servings. When you have one serving for eacl family member, heat them up, and you've got an instant dinner.

# Hire a family chef

My favorite way of treating my husband and me to an inexpensiv night off is to hire a chef—one of my children. I pay him/her fo cooking the meal, since this is outside his regular chores, and the money stays in the family.

Teach your children how to prepare several meals. Retype recip cards to indicate step-by-step instructions for preparing an entire dinner from cooking to cleanup. This will be valuable experience fo them—and you. Then come to an understanding about the price yo will pay for this extra service.

On a night when you know you'll be home late or when you just fee like taking the night off from cooking, suggest that one of your kid become chef for the night. Boys as well as girls enjoy this occasiona cooking stint and the skills they master come in very handy later in life. For some reason foreign dishes—Italian, Mexican and Chinese—are great favorites with new cooks. And these are often not too expensive to prepare. Stir-fried beef, tacos, and spaghetti are great favorites. Here's a sample beginner's recipe:

## Easy Oven-Fried Chicken

Rinse chicken parts quickly in water—pat dry with paper napkin.
Turn on oven to 400°. Put half a stick of margarine in 9″ × 13″ pan
and put in oven, close the oven door.
Put ½ cup of flour and 1 teaspoon of paprika in large size Baggie.
Put in chicken pieces and shake (hold the top of the bag or you will
get floured too!!!) so the chicken gets coated with the flour.
(use a potholder) Get the pan out of the oven and put chicken in
pan, skin side down.

*Idea:* If you want to have baked potatoes, wash a potato for each
person and put in oven—just sit on the oven rack.
Set the timer for 30 minutes. (If you go out of the kitchen, take the
timer with you so you hear it ring.)
When timer rings, get out pan and turn chicken over. Put back in
for another 30 minutes and set the timer again.
When it rings, chicken AND potatoes are ready.
Turn oven off.
Dinner is ready!

## Freezer easers

Relax, these ideas do not require that you spend every weekend
cooking and packaging all sorts of goodies to stash in the freezer. They
are just hints for quick, inexpensive freezer use. Having some ready-
to-go things in the freezer saves money because you are making
convenience items instead of buying them. You can also take advantage
of peak-of-the-season sales and make use of overripe fruits and stale
bread instead of throwing food away!

Your freezer operates more efficiently when it is full. Make a bagful
of ice cubes to keep in an empty spot in the freezer. Then you will
have them handy. Also make block ice (see page 6).

Next time you make pancakes or waffles, make a double batch.
Freeze the extras to be reheated for an instant breakfast. They can

both be reheated in the microwave or oven. Waffles can also
done in the toaster.

- If you have fresh herbs, chop them and put in an ice-cube tray. A
water to fill the cube. Freeze and then pop into a Baggie. If y
want to add parsley or whatever to a dish, just throw in a froz
cube.
- My favorite way (easy, of course) to use peaches/nectarines
apples when you get a treeful all at once:

---

### *Make-Ahead Pie Filling*

5 cups sliced fresh fruit (peaches, apples, etc.)
3 tablespoons flour
3/4 cup sugar
dash of cinnamon
Shake above ingredients in a heavy-duty plastic bag so fruit
coated with flour/sugar mixture. Squeeze out air and freez
When you want to bake a fresh fruit pie on a winter day, just ma
a pie crust, add Make-Ahead Pie Filling, and bake as usual. Tast
like just-picked fruit pie.

---

- Toss brown, overripe bananas in the freezer *in their skins*. U
them to make banana shakes in the blender or banana bread. Th
are terrific for banana daiquiris. Just peel, chop, and add froz
banana to your recipe. No one will ever know they came from t
freezer.
- Freezer ideas. Start a special section in your recipe box where y
note down ideas for using your freezer. Whenever you think o
new way to save time or money, jot it down and file it. Don't
those good ideas get away from you.
- Freezer supplies. Special freezer tape works no better than mas
ing tape, but it does cost more. Same goes for those spec
"freezer" marking pens—they are merely ordinary felt tippers
keep a felt pen and a roll of masking tape in the kitchen to use

preparing freezer packages. Freezer paper is plastic coated paper. You can put the item in a Baggie, sealing it with a twister. Then wrap in brown paper cut from grocery sacks. This seems to work as well as the special freezer paper you can buy and is certainly cheaper.

Keep track of frozen foods. Number your freezer shelves from top to bottom. You don't actually have to write numbers on the shelves, but put a note on the freezer door to remind you which shelf is which. Then do a freezer inventory. Jot down on cards everything you have in the freezer and the shelf number where it is located. When something is used, cross it off the inventory list. This saves time in locating items in the freezer, and you always know what you have on hand.

# ake your own convenience foods

If you prepare convenience foods right in your own kitchen, you'll ve money and still have the time-saving benefits these foods ovide.

Instant onions. Buy a 3-pound bag of yellow onions when the price is right. Chop and freeze them in small (sandwich bag) portions so they will be ready to use. When a recipe calls for ½ cup of chopped onion, you've got it. Works beautifully with green onions and green peppers.

Bread crumbs. In a blender or food processor (or you can use a hand cheese grater) twirl stale bread into crumbs and freeze. (These also keep well in a screw top jar in the fridge.) Then, just shake out the amount you need. It's not necessary to defrost frozen ones. Combine with your favorite herbs (try oregano or ground sage) for an extra flavor note.

Shredded cheese. Buy mozzarella or other cheese when it's on special, shred it as you would to use in a recipe, wrap it in 1 cup portions, and store it in the freezer. When you make pizza or lasagna, it is ready to use.

Frozen bread. If bread customarily gets stale before you use up the loaf, store it in the door of the freezer and just take out a few piece at a time. In our family, nobody but me likes crunchy-wheat bread so I always freeze half the loaf and use the other half. That way, doesn't get wasted.

- Avocado pulp. When avocados are at their cheapest, buy a dozen Wait till they're ripe (that's when they yield to gentle thumb pressure), scoop out the pulp and mix with lemon juice. Then freeze pulp to use when you want to make guacamole (avocado dip) Tastes just like fresh and is much cheaper than buying frozen dip.

- Ground beef. Buy ground beef when it's on sale and prepare you favorite recipes. Mix up your usual meatloaf and, instead of cooking it, freeze it in its loaf shape. Then when time is short for fixing dinner, your meatloaf is ready to bake. (Caution: For using frozen items this large and solid, you must plan ahead. As you get ready to leave for work in the morning, take the meatloaf out of the freezer and put it in the refrigerator to defrost.)

   Meatballs can also be frozen. Mix and freeze them on a cookie sheet until firm, then put them in a container and freeze. Or freeze ground patties for instant burgers. They can be fried or grilled while still frozen, for an instant meal or snack.

- Big batches. Prepare food in large amounts, and store half (or more) for later use. When you prepare an extra large batch, you don't spend much more time than in preparing a small one, and you save on energy used in cooking. The best part of all is knowing you have items tucked away in your freezer that are ready to go.

- Chocolate chip cookies (or any other unfrosted cookies) can be baked and frozen. Make three times as many as usual and freeze the extra batches. To stop your children from raiding the freezer and finding all these goodies, mismark the package. A label like "liver" will keep them from touching it.

- Banana bread (or any fruit bread) can be baked and frozen. Bake several loaves at once to save energy. For a small family, cut the loaves in half before freezing, so you can use half a loaf at a time.

- Frozen cooked roast. Roast two or three rump roasts at once. Slice and freeze the extras with gravy.

- Frozen baked chicken. Buy 4 whole chickens on special. Put all four chickens in a big roaster pan and bake. Bake for about 90 minutes at 350° or till done. Remove meat from the bones and freeze four packets of cooked chicken meat to use in salads or dishes requiring cooked chicken. Combine bones with water, onion and herbs and simmer for about an hour for delectable, low-cost chicken broth.

- Entire meal. Save energy by cooking the entire meal in the oven. Roast beef, baked potatoes, and a frozen veggie can all cook at once. To cook a frozen vegetable in the oven, dump it into an ovenproof dish, add some water and a dab of butter, cover and bake for twenty minutes.

## Saving on lunches

Eating out is costly. If you spend $1 a day on snacks, that adds up to over $200 a year. When my sister Dianne wanted to cut calories and costs she decided that instead of lunching out every day, she would take lunch four days a week and eat out just once, in mid-week. For snacks at work, she keeps in her office a mug, instant coffee and hot chocolate, and a plug-in hot pot (cost $10). Instead of buying snacks from vending machines or from the snack wagon, she fixes herself a hot drink and gets an apple or bran muffin out of her briefcase.

## Breakfast ideas

- Make your own yogurt. A yogurt maker costs about $12 and you'll quickly recover the cost of purchase by making your own much less expensive and equally tasty supplies. Add lightly sweetened fresh berries and other fruits and you'll also save on calories. A cup of yogurt makes a great summer breakfast (winter too). Also, yogurt is a great base for blender drinks (see below).
- Apple oatmeal. Make oatmeal in your usual manner except add a dash of cinnamon, a handful of raisins, and sliced apples. Tastes terrific and costs a lot less than instant-oatmeal packets.

- Cottage cheese with fruit (or without).
- Wheat toast with peanut butter.
- PB and J (that's a peanut butter and jelly sandwich—who says you can't eat it for breakfast?).
- Breakfast in a glass. Mix or blend up a nutritious breakfast drink. I keep these recipes on a shelf right by the blender so my kids can mix drinks themselves. Use those frozen bananas in these recipes. Chop them into chunks before putting them in the blender.
    1. cup yogurt (plain)
       1 banana
       ½ cup orange juice
       1 or 2 tablespoons wheat germ
       Blend and drink.
    2. yogurt
       fruit
       2 ice cubes
       Blend and drink.
    3. 1 banana
       1 cup milk
       1 egg
       1 teaspoon vanilla
       Blend and drink.
    4. 1 cup orange juice
       1 egg
       Blend and drink.
    5. fruit (use any of these: peaches, berries, bananas, papayas, apricots)
       milk or yogurt
       Blend and drink.

## Making the most of meat

Dinner is usually the most expensive meal to prepare because of the cost of meat. Meat costs can be reduced by clever shopping and meal-preparation techniques. Since most Americans eat too much meat anyway (according to the American Heart Association), use less. Put more vegetables and less meat in your stir-fry dishes. Cut down on the ground beef in your spaghetti sauce. I did, and no one noticed. Using less meat cuts costs and makes a more healthful meal.

- Check the cookbooks in your local library (you can find them in the section numbered 641). Review the books that specialize in low-cost or meatless meals/recipes. Some public libraries have photo-copying machines so you can simply copy the recipes you like. But if you're in a rush and can't review the books until you get home, you can write out recipes you like.

- Become a parttime butcher in your own kitchen. You can save lots of money if you learn a few meat-cutting secrets from the pros. Several excellent meat cookbooks are now available in paperback or in your public library. These show how to cut your meat step-by-step, so that you can make the most of such inexpensive cuts as chuck steak.

- If you are trying to decide which cut of meat is better for a particular dish you want to prepare, ask the butcher. Or if you see a package of meat with a temptingly low price per pound, but you are not sure how to use it, ring the buzzer. The butcher may have a great idea for preparing that particular cut of meat. Another way of getting terrific money-saving recipes is to ask other shoppers. If you see someone buying something, ask her how to prepare it. That's how I've found out about some of our favorite dishes.

## Seasonings and sauces

Can special seasoning packets turn a plain cook into a gourmet chef? The answer is no. And those small foil packets of spices and season-ings are usually much more expensive than regular spices. If you like a special seasoning blend, read the ingredients on the foil packet and make yourself a jarful to keep in your cupboard. Stop yourself when you reach for a 50¢ package of taco seasoning just because you are making a Mexican meal.

- Recipes from Barbara Jean's kitchen.

## BARBECUE SAUCE/MARINADE.

Brush on chicken or spareribs while baking or barbecuing.

Mix or stir together
1 cup catsup
⅓ cup vinegar
¼ cup sugar
⅓ cup soy sauce
1 tablespoon chili powder

## TERIYAKI SAUCE/MARINADE.

Marinate chicken or beef in this Oriental style sauce and then bake, broil or barbecue for a delicious treat. You can also stir-fry flank steak strips after marinating for several hours for an interesting variation.

Mix or stir together
½ cup soy sauce
¼ cup vegetable oil
3 tablespoons dry sherry
¼ to ½ teaspoon ground ginger
1 small clove garlic, minced
2 tablespoons brown sugar

## MEXICAN SAUCE.

Use for making beef burritos.

Sauté
1 - 1½ pounds ground beef
1 cup chopped celery
1 large onion, chopped

Add
>   2 8-ounce cans tomato sauce
>   1 8-ounce can mild green-chili salsa

Heat and spoon on a flour tortilla. (Optional: You can add shredded jack cheese and/or sliced avocado.) Roll and eat.


### BARBECUE SAUCE.


Use for making barbecue beef buns. Can also be used as sauce or marinade for beef, chicken, or spareribs.

>   Sauté in 2 tablespoons oil or margarine
>>       chopped onion
>>       chopped green pepper (optional)
>>       1 clove garlic, minced
>   Add
>>       1½ cups catsup
>>       2 tablespoons Worcestershire
>>       3 tablespoons brown sugar
>>       3 tablespoons mustard

Add sauteed ground beef (1 pound) and serve in French rolls or hamburger buns.

* Spice it up. Try buying spices in bulk form. You can get them for bargain prices. For years I ordered them by mail from:

      Charles Loeb Distributors
      615 Palmer Road
      Yonkers, NY 10701

Write for a price list and ask if they have a minimum order. If so, find some friends and neighbors who might like to share a pound bag of spices. You do have to pay for shipping, so put together a big order and share the wealth with friends, relatives, neighbors, or co-workers.

  I no longer order spices by mail, because I can get them through my food co-op (see page 131) at the same prices without delivery charges. Look in the Yellow Pages of your phone book to see if any one in your area sells bulk spices.

• Flavored rice and noodle mixes. One 8-ounce package of flavored rice may cost as much as a 28-ounce bag of plain rice. And all you are really getting is a box of precooked rice with a seasoning packet. The seasoning packet contains a bouillon cube and a spoonful of curry powder (or whatever). You can easily make your own interesting rice mixes. Here are four recipes for Tastyrice and four recipes for Supernoodles.

### TASTYRICE 1

Melt 2 tablespoons butter or margarine.
Add chopped onion and sauté.
Add water, 2 chicken bouillon cubes, and dash of ground thyme.
Cook rice as usual.

### TASTYRICE 2

Substitute beef bouillon cubes for the chicken in recipe 1 for a different flavor. Our family enjoys them both.

### TASTYRICE 3

Cook rice in your usual manner.
Sauté in melted butter or margarine ¼ cup each of minced parsley and minced green onions. Add to rice for a delicious, colorful rice dish.

## TASTYRICE 4

Melt 2 tablespoons butter or margarine.
Add and sauté
    ½ cup chopped celery
    1 chopped onion
    sliced mushrooms (if you happen to have some)
    salt, pepper, and pinch of dillweed.
Add rice, water, and 2 bouillon cubes (beef or chicken) and cook
rice in your usual manner.

## SUPERNOODLES 1

Melt 3 tablespoons butter or margarine.
Add 2 chicken bouillon cubes and ¼ cup sesame seeds. Sauté till
seeds are golden brown. Pour over cooked noodles and stir till
mixed.

## SUPERNOODLES 2

Substitute ¼ cup poppy seeds for the sesame seeds.

## SUPERNOODLES 3

Omit seeds and add 1 tablespoon paprika.

## SUPERNOODLES 4

Omit seeds and use ½ cup slivered almonds instead. Sauté them
in the butter.

Fresh parsley makes a perfect garnish for Tastyrice or Supernoodles. Chop and sprinkle on top before serving.

- Salad dressings. These easy-to-fix dressing recipes all start with the same two ingredients—mayonnaise and lemon juice. Mixing your own dressings is more economical than bottled salad dressings; your better-tasting dressings are free of chemical additives ("for pourability"). Mix in a bowl, food processor, or blender, cover and refrigerate.

### INSTANT FRENCH

1 cup mayonnaise
2 tablespoons lemon juice
1 tablespoon milk
1 tablespoon sugar
salt and pepper
1 teaspoon paprika
dash of dry mustard

### INSTANT BLUE CHEESE

1 cup mayonnaise
2 tablespoons lemon juice
¼ cup milk
2 teaspoons sugar
dash Worcestershire sauce
salt and pepper
crumbled blue cheese (I use the cheapest wedge, about 4 ounces, I can find in the store)

### INSTANT ITALIAN (THE CREAMY KIND)

1 cup mayonnaise
2 tablespoons lemon juice
3 tablespoons milk
2 tablespoons vinegar (any kind)
salt and pepper
1/2 teaspoon sugar
1 teaspoon mixed Italian seasonings (dried) or dried oregano

# Cleanup tactics

One reason for eating dinner out when you'd really rather stay at home is that there are no dishes to do. Try to streamline kitchen cleanup so you are not tempted to dash out for fast food.

- For an instant cleanup, fill a bowl or pan that was used in fixing the meal with hot, sudsy water. As you prepare the meal, put all utensils in the water to soak during mealtime. After the meal, family members carry their dishes and utensils to the sink area. Utensils go in the "soak container," and the dishes are rinsed and put in a dishpan of sudsy water or in the dishwasher. Makes cleanup much faster.

- The team cleanup is the fastest technique yet, guaranteeing that no family member is left to clean up the kitchen alone. Upon finishing the meal, all family members stay on the scene and participate in the team cleanup. Dishes are washed and dried, the trash is dumped, the dog gets fed, and lunches are packed for tomorrow. (Our family record for the cleanup is 12 minutes—not bad for a family of six.) It sure makes eating at home more inviting.

- A good snacktime strategy is to insist that family members wash snack dishes right away. This eliminates kitchen clutter and means fewer dishes to do following a meal. Assign each family member a different color mug and matching plate, so they can use their own equipment for snacks—you'll have fewer dishes to wash and possibly fewer broken dishes.

# 2

# BUYING BEAUTIFUL BARGAIN CLOTHES

It's possible to have a terrific wardrobe without spending a fortune. Very often the people with the greatest flair and style are simply smart shoppers, who plan not only what they are going to buy but where they can get it for the best price. They choose clothes that fit into their existing wardrobes *and* work for many different occasions. Usually, with just a bit of thought and some imaginative accessorizing, you can build a super wardrobe from the basics that are already hanging in your closet. The secret is to do some analyzing and organizing before you buy another thing.

## BASIC TACTICS

Building a beautiful bargain-priced wardrobe is as simple as one, two, three:

1. analyze
2. organize
3. shop smart

# Analyze your wardrobe needs

- Think about how and where you spend most of your time. What kind of clothing do you wear most? Do you usually need casual, dressy, or tailored clothing? When I was a full-time homemaker, busy with a bunch of toddlers, my daily "uniform" was casual pants, jeans, T-shirts, and sweaters. Then when I began teaching elementary school, I added casual skirts, sweaters, blouses, and blazers to my wardrobe to mix and match into nice-looking outfits. Now, as a lecturer and public-relations person, I need a career wardrobe of good blouses and skirted suits. My clothing needs are certainly different from what they were when I stayed at home or taught school. When you pinpoint the type of clothing you wear most, you will know exactly where to spend most of your clothing budget.
- Take out your favorite outfit and try to figure out why you like it and wear it so much. Ask yourself exactly why this particular outfit is a "winner." Is it because of the color, fabric, style? My most-worn outfit is actually a group of coordinated separates, a toast-brown corduroy skirt, blazer, and pants. I like the style, color, and fit, and have a bunch of blouses and sweaters that look terrific with it. No wonder I wear these so often. Once you identify your own most

popular outfit, consider buying another one that is similar but in a different color or fabric. Chances are that you will wear it as often as your first favorite. This is one of the prime secrets of shopping smart—start paying attention to what you like and then go buy it.

# Organize—take a clothing inventory

- Pull everything (yes, everything) out of your closet and chest of drawers. A good time to tackle this project is a rainy weekend. Turn on your favorite music, make a pot of tea or coffee, and tear into that wardrobe. This exercise generally reveals all sorts of hidden treasures. Sort out your clothing into stacks of sweaters, blouses, skirts, pants, dresses, and suits, so you'll get a better idea of just what you own in the way of clothing.

- Then reorganize it. Start with your closet. By adding just a few closet organizers, you will better utilize the closet space you have available (is there ever enough?). When your closet is organized, you can quickly find what you want. And let's face it, if you can't find a garment, you certainly can't wear it.

- Once you've got everything sorted into stacks, list various categories of clothing on file cards: all your blouses on one card, sweaters on another card, skirts, pants, suits and blazers, and so on. Tuck the cards into an envelope and keep it in a handy spot. When you buy something new, add it to your wardrobe list.

  Take your closet inventory cards with you when you go shopping. When trying to make up your mind about a blouse color, you can look at the list of blouses you already own. The other good part about listing all the things you have is that you will discover the "holes" in your wardrobe. You can add a blouse or sweater in a certain color and gain several more switch-around outfits. In other words, the inventory shows you what you have and what you need.

- Stop! Don't put anything back in your closet that hasn't been worn in the past year. If a year has gone by without a wearing, chances are you won't ever wear that garment again. Sad—but you know it's true. Look at the clothing you never wear, the "losers" in your wardrobe. Attempt to determine why you don't wear these particular items, in order to avoid making similar purchases in the future.

> Is it too small?
> Is it too big?
> If it's not flattering, why is that true?
> Is it trendy and outdated?
> Is it a poor color for you?
> Did you buy it just because it was on sale?
> Did you buy it in a rush?

• **Four ways to cope with clothes mistakes.** If you've let those "never-worns" hang in your closet for years, you've missed some great opportunities for creative problem-solving. Here are four possible solutions:

**Alter it.** If it fits poorly and you're certain that's all that turns you off, get it altered. If you sew, do easy alterations yourself. Or take it to an expert. Check on the price of alterations first, at least to get some "ballpark figures." Never put garments that need alterations back in the closet, or you will probably forget all about them again. Either keep them in view as a reminder or dispose of them.

**Give it away.** Give never-worn garments to a friend or relative. A dark-gold blouse I once bought looked fine with two of my suits, but it was not a flattering color for me. So I gave it to a friend who looks wonderful in it and wears it often.

**Sell it.** Garage sales and flea markets (see pages 127–130) are good outlets for used garments. Or you could try selling them to a thrift shop or secondhand store. You will not make a great deal of money selling used clothing, but anything is better than taking a complete loss on those garments you never wear.

**Make a donation to a charity.** The Salvation Army and Goodwill Industries accept used clothing. Donations to nonprofit organizations are tax deductible, so it will pay in terms of income-tax savings. You can deduct "current cash value" of each item. Current cash value means the amount of money you could sell the item for . To get those prices, stroll through a secondhand store or flea market and note what similar garments are selling for. Then keep track of the number of items you donate and get a receipt for tax purposes.

# Shopping Savvy

Once you've assessed your needs, you can approach shopping the way those professional shoppers do. You'll know exactly what you're looking for and you'll make fewer mistakes and many more brilliant sale buys.

## Shop smart

- Start a clothes idea file. Clip fashion ideas that you like from magazines, even if it's only an unusual color combination. This can be a great source of ideas for putting together separates, combining colors, and using accessories in a way you might not have thought of on your own.
- Avoid spur-of-the-moment purchases, unless it's something you absolutely know is right for you. If you have any doubt, don't buy it. Often impulse buys are things you would not have purchased if you'd thought it through.
- Buy clothing that fits well. Alterations can be pricy, so when you know you will have to have a garment altered, add the alteration costs to the price of the garment you're considering for purchase.
- Dress for what you're shopping for. Have you ever tried on a wool suit while wearing jogging shoes? Take it from me, it looks funny and throws off your sense of judgment. So wear the shoes you'll wear with whatever you are shopping for. Pay attention to hair and makeup, too, so you can tell how clothing will look and not make an expensive mistake.
- Figure prices on a cost-per-wearing basis. If you buy a wool suit for $160 and wear it twenty times this winter, that boils down to a cost of $8 per wearing. A $50 cocktail dress that you wear twice costs $25 each wearing. Therefore, the wool suit at $160 is actually cheaper than the cocktail dress at $50, because it is worn more often. That is why you should spend more money on the clothing you get the most wear from. Spend less on clothing that is high

fashion, trendy stuff that quickly goes out of style—or don't buy it at all.

- When to shop:

    Shop early in the season to get the best *choice*.

    Shop late in the season to get the best *price*.

    I bought my favorite wool suit in mid-July when the store was just putting out the winter clothes. That is when the selection is most extensive, and since wool suits are for wearing to work, I wanted to be sure to get just what I wanted. For less important garments, I wait until the end-of-season sales and save money. The choice is more limited—often common sizes are all but gone—but if I find something, it is usually a bargain.

- Usually if you're not sure you want a garment, don't buy it. It's not a good idea to get into the habit of making purchases with the idea that you can take them back. We often find that we don't take them back. However, if you like something but aren't sure about the color matching something at home or *if* you're pretty sure you want something or *if* the store is very close to your home, it is generally a good idea to take the item, which might be gone if you waited.

## Sale survival tactics

Sale shopping can be a wonderful way to get major items like coats, raincoats, and suits at bargain prices. Also, you can often pick up beautiful accessories at end-of-the-season sales. But sales also tempt you to spend money on "bargains" you don't need, so follow my survival tips for smart sale shopping.

- Shop a sale the evening before. Most stores mark down sale items the evening before the sale really starts. My daughter Sue worked in a high-priced department store one summer. I was all set to hit their sale on the first day for which it was advertised, when she called me from work: "Don't wait for tomorrow, Mother. Everything has been marked down and is being sold at sale prices this evening." What a revelation! Now I know that almost all the stores do that. You don't have to fight the mob on sale day if you go the evening before.

- Get on a mailing list. Some stores have preferred-customer sales when certain customers (usually those with the store's charge account) get to buy merchandise before it is on sale to the general public. If your favorite stores have preferred customer days—call them and ask—get on their mailing list so you receive these notices.
- Ask about upcoming sales. When you are ready to make a purchase, ask the salesperson if the item will soon be on sale. If the salesperson is not sure, talk to the department manager. When I learned that all junior dresses were going to be 30 percent off in a few days, I held off making my purchases. It never hurts to ask.
- Sales merchandise is usually rather small in quantity and rather large in size. If you wear large sizes, you may do much better at sales than your size 10 friends.
- Carry the announcement of the sale with you, from a newspaper or a mail advertisement. You can thus make certain you are getting the sale price and that you are seeing all the sale merchandise.
- Sales clothes are only a bargain when you need the item, know it will be worn, and are certain it works with your existing wardrobe. You are not saving a penny if you buy something you would not have bought otherwise.
- To be ready to take advantage of sales you might suddenly spot, carry a small notebook containing a list of your family's sizes and wardrobe requirements, plus your own wardrobe-inventory cards.

## The best times to shop

- Shop at good-mood times. When you are angry, frustrated, or bored, don't go shopping. Buy a magazine or crossword puzzle book instead—something that will give you the momentary lift you crave—and you'll avoid the possibility of making a serious shopping mistake.
- Avoid last-minute searches. If you need an outfit for some special event, shop early and give yourself plenty of time. Shopping for a dress or other outfit that you *must* have *that very night* puts you under an intolerable pressure.

- Shop for shoes late in the day when your feet tend to be at their maximum size. If the shoes are comfortable then, they will probably always be comfortable. Breaking in painful shoes is not worth the effort, and you tend to end up with a heap of unusable footwear.
- Give yourself time to decide. If you see something you like but want to shop around a bit more, put the items on hold. Most stores will hold garments for a few hours or until closing time that day. This gives you time to shop around a bit more before making your decision. If you decide you do not want the item, the store will take it off hold when the time is up—you don't have to return to the store to tell them. If you spot something you think a family member or friend might want but are not sure, put the garment on hold and telephone the person about your find.

## Sales people

- If you find a salesperson you like jot down his/her name for future reference. You'd be amazed at how valuable such a relationship can be. You can learn about bargains and upcoming sales and just generally have an extra pair of eyes searching out clothes that might be right for you. Make a point to bring such helpers a holiday treat or other thank-you gift from time to time.
- Hold your own. Don't be intimidated by haughty salespersons. In high-priced stores, take your time, look through the clothes, don't hesitate to try things on to see how certain styles look on you. If the price is too high, you have the right to decide you don't want the garment after all.

## Good points to remember

- Don't shop with your kids. Shop alone or with an adult shopping companion. Children take your attention away from the task in hand, and you're much more likely to make a mistake when you're distracted or rushed. Leave the youngsters at home if you possibly can.

- A discount-buying guide for your geographic area is a useful thing to have on hand. Thanks to such a handy paperback book about bargain hunting in my area, I've located several great spots to shop. Check your local bookstore.
- Leather goods can be deceptive. Often pricy shoes or handbags, sold in the finest department stores, are not real leather but leather-look plastic. Check inside the shoes or bag to see if it is stamped "real leather" or "man-made materials." The latter does not look, feel, or wear as well as leather. Even salespeople may just assume an item is leather because it looks like it. So check for yourself.
- Look and compare before you buy. To make maximum use of discount stores, I shop first in the very best department stores for ideas. Then I zip to the discount store to buy. That way I'm prepared to spot a bargain when I see one. Some discount stores have a "no returns" policy, so shop carefully.
- Cleaning costs count, too. Check the information on the labels that tell how to care for the garment before you buy it. If it must be dry-cleaned, keep the cleaning costs in mind. You might telephone a dry cleaner and get a price on having a silk dress (or whatever) cleaned before you make the purchase. Then at least you will know what to expect.
- If you wear a small women's size, check the clothing in teen and boys' departments. A preppy-look polo shirt and button-down shirt costs much less in those departments than a similar item in a woman's department.
- To make returns easier, leave tags on garments until you are ready to wear them for the first time. Also, always save receipts. Then returns are easy if you should change your mind or find yourself dissatisfied with a purchase. (See page 147 for how to get what you want when you are a dissatisfied customer.)
- When panty hose get a run, I mark an x with a laundry marker pen inside the waistband elastic. That reminds me that that pair has a run and to wear them with slacks.
- To extend the life of panty hose with runs, cut off the leg that has the run in it. When you have two pair of one-legged pantyhose, put

them on. If they are the kind with "tummy control" like I buy, you have double tummy control and your panty hose look just fine.

## Color—key to a cost-efficient wardrobe

- Plan your wardrobe around two or three basic colors. Basics are either neutral or dark colors that you can wear with many other colors. So even if bright red is your favorite, you'd be wise to choose navy and gray as your basics and use reds only as accent colors. You would buy jackets, pants, and skirts in your basic colors, and blouses, sweaters, and scarves in accent colors. Your navy suit would look fabulous with a red print blouse, a wine sweater, or a rose-colored silk shirt. If you have money to buy just one suit, buy it in a solid, basic color that you will wear with pleasure for several years.
- Shop in half of your outfit. Wear your skirt or pants when you are shopping for a blouse to wear with it. Don't trust your memory when matching or blending colors. Trying on the pieces together is the best way to find out if the color and style are right.
- Make sure you have the right color. I once saw sweaters on sale and could not make up my mind if the navy or burgundy would be the more versatile in my wardrobe. I bought them both knowing that I would be returning one of them. Then I went home, made my decision, and returned one sweater to the store.
- If you are looking for leather goods in a go-with-everything color, buy taupe. Taupe (brownish gray) looks wonderful with black, white, or any color. You might even buy two pairs of taupe shoes, one in a sling-back style and one in a classic closed shoe. This is a color that spans the seasons as well as complementing every color, so it is a bargain-hunter's dream.

## Classic clothes never go out of style

- Classic casuals like jeans, shirts, crew or v-neck sweaters, and denim skirts always stay in style. Buy colors you can mix and match for a multitude of great sporty looks.

- Suits with skirts are a perfect business look. In the right style and fabric, they can be very feminine looking. A classic suit equals several outfits because you can wear it with many different blouses and sweaters. A one-piece dress equals one outfit. If you need a business wardrobe, spend the extra money for a suit.
- Try on suits with short and long jackets. Decide which jacket length looks best on you. Most short women look better in shorter jackets—long jackets make them appear big and boxy. Tall women, on the other hand, benefit from the shortening effect of long jackets.
- Blazers are highly wearable, versatile investments, wearable with either slacks or skirts. I prefer wool blazers to corduroy because corduroy shows wear at the elbows. However, you can add leather elbow patches to sporty corduroy blazers, and they look terrific. Blazers are always in style.
- Shirt dresses are another classic style that makes for a good investment. I have one in a wool challis and another in silk that I've been wearing for at least three years. Far as I'm concerned, I'll still be wearing them three years from now. They simply don't go out of style.
- Stick with the style you like. When you find something you really like, buy it in several colors. I do this all the time with blouses, sweaters, and shoes. When you like something a lot, you wear it a lot and get your money's worth, so why not recognize this and avoid offbeat mistakes?
- Buy coordinates for a pulled-together look. If you are buying two pieces like a skirt and blazer, buy the matching slacks, too. That will expand the number of different looks you can get from your coordinates.
- When a man buys a suit, he should buy an extra pair of matching pants whenever possible. Because the pants get worn far more often than the jacket, having two pairs of the matching trousers will lengthen the life of the suit.
- Avoid faddy or trendy clothes. It's fun to buy things that are the very newest look, of course, but when the trend fades, you have something you don't want to wear because it looks dated.

- Designer labels usually cost more—a lot more. What is it worth to you to have someone's name or monogram on the back pocket of your pants? Nondesigner jeans wear as well as name brands.

  But designer coats and suits can be a great buy if you shop the discount stores or end-of-season sales. I've bought some at super-deal prices.

# Shopping by mail

Long-distance shopping can save time and money.

- No-fit items like sheets, blankets, bedding, towels, or easy-fit ones like socks, robes, and underwear are ideal for ordering from money-saving catalogs. If you order by phone, your order can be picked up in person at the catalog desk of the retail store (if there is one). Otherwise, check delivery costs so you know what to expect.
- Look in the newspaper, then the phone book. Order items advertised in the newspaper by telephone. Many department stores have an advertising booklet in the Sunday newspaper. You can order their merchandise and charge it to your account. Find out if there is a delivery fee.
- Where to deliver is often a problem to a working person. If there is no one at home during the day, have merchandise you order delivered to your work address. (You will then have to lug it home, of course.) Or if you have an obliging neighbor, ask her to receive the item for you—either at her own house or, if it's a massive object, let the deliveryman into yours.
- Keep a copy of the order form, date ordered, and company's address when you buy through the mail. Then you will have all the information necessary to check up on the order, if you have to. I make a note on my calendar on the date by which I expect to receive the merchandise, so I don't forget about it. When you receive your merchandise, compare the contents of the package with your copy of the order form, to verify that you have received everything you ordered.

# How to keep your kids in clothes without going bankrupt

- Order a bunch of name tapes to sew into jackets and sweaters. Have your last name only printed on the tapes, and you can use them for all family members. Or write the name inside clothing with a waterproof laundry marker. Sew tapes into all outer garments— even adult raincoats (easy to misplace since many are identical or look it). Children often do not recognize their own jackets if they are not marked. I speak from experience on this subject because when I was an elementary school teacher, we had a heap of jackets and sweaters in the coat corner that my students swore they had never seen before. Yet all had been worn in by class members.

- Save worn-out tennis shoes for creek-walking, playing in the rain and other watery activities (climbing on rocks on the beach). My sixteen-year-old son still has a pair of "creek-walkers" he uses on occasion.

- Treat yourself to a thrift shop shopping tour. You'll be pleasantly surprised at the treasures you will find at rock bottom prices. Some stores specialize in children's clothing. Quickly outgrown, little-worn items such as fancy baby and toddler outfits, ice skates, and ski jackets abound. Thrift shops carry clothing for every member of the family. Look in the Yellow Pages under *Clothing, Used* to locate thrift shops in your area. Check them out—you'll be glad you did. Many shoppers in the thrift stores have money to shop elsewhere, they simply know a good deal when they see one. That's what I call smart shopping.

- Buy secondhand clothes for one-time wear. When your child needs an outfit to wear only once, buy it used. My son had to wear a suit (oh, no!) for junior-high graduation. I knew he would wear that suit one time only and it seemed an awful waste of money to buy him a new one. Instead, I purchased a beautiful navy blazer for six dollars at a secondhand clothing store. Well, that six-dollar blazer has been worn by all three boys in our family to a bar mitzvah, several weddings, and two graduations. When my youngest boy outgrew it, I gave it to a neighbor who needed a graduation get-up for her son.

- Never talk your child into buying something he/she does not like. Believe me, clothes bought under pressure don't get worn.
- Set up a school uniform exchange. Because school uniforms are usually expensive and some kids outgrow them in a short time, a school-uniform exchange can be a great money saver. All it takes is a spot on the school bulletin board where parents can post items they want to sell or buy. Or perhaps people who wish to buy or sell uniforms could be listed in the monthly school newsletter. Most parents are delighted to recover some of the money they spend on uniforms when they don't have younger children to pass them on to.
- Exchange kids' outgrown clothing. Young children outgrow clothing so quickly, it's often just like new. Set up a periodic swap meet at the beginning of every season, at which you exchange your youngsters' outgrown garments with friends or relatives.
- Buy one for now and one to grow on. When you see jackets or sweaters at a supersaver price, consider buying one for your child for immediate use and one in a larger size for next year. You can almost count on them costing more next year.
- Iron patches on the *inside* of brand-new pants before they are worn. Then the knees are double strength, thanks to the "invisible patches" on the inside.
- For super-quick, low-cost nylon repairs, buy a package of adhesive, nylon repair fabric. It will fix tears in nylon jackets, duffel bags, backpacks, and sleeping bags. You can locate this handy product in the sporting-goods section of a variety store, usually selling for less than $2. Each package contains several colors of nylon adhesive patches, which you can just cut and put on like a Band-Aid. These are also perfect for mending tears in down jackets or coats.
- When your kids wear out a pair of jeans or corduroy pants, cut yourself several patches from the back of the pants legs before throwing them away. Then you will have a variety of sew-on patches for free. (Since my kids tend to wear navy blue or tan corduroy or standard blue jeans, often I can use the patches on same-fabric clothing where they're almost invisible.)
- When your child finds an iron-on decal in a cereal box or in a magazine and isn't sure how it will look, iron it on a pillowcase

instead of a t-shirt. Then if it isn't a rave success, it doesn't matter. But if you put that decal on a t-shirt, it's almost a sure thing he/she will stop wearing the shirt.

## Caring for your clothes

- Air your clothing the way grandma did. Instead of having your wool suit or coat cleaned because it smells like smoke, hang it by a window or outdoors to air. Then return it to your closet.
- Instead of overheating blouses, sweaters, robes and nightgowns in the dryer, hang them up on tubular plastic hangers. Adds life to garments and saves electricity too.
- To preserve delicate fabrics, buy a mesh bag to wash delicate items. I wash my nylon pantyhose that way, and it works beautifully. Then just drape over a plastic hanger to dry.
- When washing garments with Velcro closures, make certain that Velcro flaps are closed, so that the rough closure surfaces do not damage other delicate fabrics. My bathing suit was once ruined by a Velcro closure on a pair of boys' pants—it made snags and pulls all over the bathing suit fabric.
- When synthetic-blend clothing becomes marred by hard-to-lift grease stains, run them through a bulk, by-the-pound dry cleaner. The cleaning process will remove many of the stains. Then run them through the washer as usual.
- Take your dry-clean-only clothing to a coin-operated dry cleaner. Or find out if your dry cleaner will take clothing "by the pound." This is a supersaver way of getting a stack of cleaning done at rock-bottom prices.
- Have garments *cleaned only* instead of cleaned and pressed. It costs less. You can touch up at home with a steam iron.
- To make sure two pieces of a suit stay the same color, get them cleaned at the same time, every time. If you get the pants cleaned repeatedly without the jacket, they will not look the same.
- Watch for "special sales" at your dry cleaners. Recently my cleaner had a one-cent sale, when they cleaned a second similar garment for 1¢. I took piles of stuff in to be cleaned in pairs: two down jackets, two silk dresses, two suits, and so on.

Dry cleaning is not only expensive; it can wear clothes out if it's done too often. To avoid frequent cleaning, use spot cleaning methods at home, let clothes rest between wearings, and air clothes in a well-ventilated place to restore shape and freshness.

Spray garments with fabric protector. Most coats, jackets, and raincoats will wear better and need less frequent cleaning if you spray them with a fabric protector (check the container to see which fabrics can be sprayed and the proper steps to follow).

Empty pockets of pants, coats, and jackets before you hang them up.

Use broad or padded hangers to hang coats and suits. Pants or skirt hangers also prolong the life of the garment.

Read and follow directions on detergents for preliminary soaking, stain removal, and when not to dry in the sun.

If you hang clothes outdoors to dry, turn them inside out to prevent sun fading.

Use a mild dishwashing detergent to wash wool and synthetic sweaters, and save money on special wool wash products.

When washing light-colored or white sweaters in lukewarm water, add a few drops of ammonia to brighten them.

## 3

# AFFORDABLE DECORATING WITH AN AFFLUENT LOOK

To achieve a great look in your apartment or house, you don't have t
spend large amounts of money or start off with treasured famil
heirlooms. All you need is your own common sense, some easy-to
acquire knowledge about the best places to shop, and some time t
plan and find out what you really want. Often the handsomest apart

ents and houses are put together by people who were working with
ıited budgets but with unlimited imaginations. If you proceed one
ep at a time, you can transform your own home into an environment
at really suits you and your family and looks terrific too.

# Basics

Before you can start decorating a house, or even a single room,
u'll need to create a plan. Start slowly, look around, study the model
oms in department stores and magazines, and you'll soon begin to
ıve a stronger sense of what you want. Most people have a general
ea of styles and colors they like, but when they have to actually
end money and make a final choice they can get pretty uptight. Since
u'll have to live with your decisions for quite a while, take your time
ıd get to know what's out there.

## planning notebook

Set aside some time to think about the people who live in your
home. How many adults and how many children have to be
accommodated? What are their interests? Do you have pets? Use a
small notebook or legal pad and write the name of each room on a
separate page. Then list under each room the people who use it and
the activities they take part in there. You'll get a much better idea of
what you need to do to make your rooms more comfortable and
more attractive when you plot things on paper.
What activities take place in the room? What you do there will
govern what you'll want to have in the way of furniture, lighting, and
so on.

## lea sources

Take full advantage of all free sources of ideas and advice that are
erywhere around you. Start a file folder or add an envelope to your

planning notebook to save photos, color chips, fabric samples, source
of products. Here are five bountiful sources of decorating ideas:

- **Magazines and newspapers.** These provide a wealth of ideas i
  full color. The furniture-store ad booklets that come with th
  Sunday newspaper are chock-full of great ideas. When you see a
  idea you like, snip it and save it for your idea folder. Look carefull
  at advertisements. I got the idea for molding and wallpaper for ou
  kitchen from a magazine ad for floor wax. You won't be copying an
  of the rooms exactly as they are shown. Instead you can pick an
  choose ideas from here and there and incorporate them into you
  decor.

- **Furniture stores and model homes.** These often have roor
  displays that are extremely helpful. Take a notebook along and you
  camera. Snap photos of room arrangements, color combinations
  and wall decorations you like. I've picked up some of my favorit
  ideas by strolling through room displays in stores and model homes

- **Advertising brochures and catalogs.** Merchandising materi
  is packed with ideas. Look through a magazine for ads that offer a
  idea booklet you can send for. The "idea booklet" shows more abou
  the product that is being advertised, usually in full color.

  Some companies charge for their idea booklets, which are reall
  advertising. I ignore the fact that the booklet costs $2 and send fo
  it without enclosing money. Most of the time, I receive the catalo
  free of charge. (My policy is *never* to pay for advertising.) We ar
  thinking about updating our thirty-year-old bathrooms, so I sen
  away for idea booklets from bathroom-fixture companies and ce
  ramic tile manufacturers and have a bunch of free materials that ar
  loaded with terrific ideas to adapt.

- **Talented friends and relatives.** Do you know someone who ha
  an eye for color or who has done an outstanding job of decoratin
  her/his own home? Ask for her assistance. Chances are she will b
  flattered that you value her opinion. You will have the pleasure o
  working with a friend. If the friend really knocks herself out, yo
  may want to buy her a small gift or treat her to lunch or dinner.

- **Decorators.** These professionals can provide service in man
  different ways. Ask about the cost of their service during the firs

minute or two of your conversation. Find out if they charge for their services by the hour. Their fee will be reflected in the cost of the items you purchase through the decorator, or you will pay by the hour. If you pay by the hour, find out exactly how the fee-schedule works. I once used a decorator to buy carpeting for me. Much to my horror she charged me by the minute for the phone call she made to order my carpeting and also charged me by the minute for a visit to my home to check the carpet installation. The fact that I was surprised was my own fault—I should have asked for an explanation of her fees right at the beginning. I was happy with the carpeting but did not continue to use the decorator. Her charges were simply too high.

Many furniture stores have "decorators" available for free. These people are really furniture salespeople, but many of them are quite talented at interior decoration. I have received excellent advice and gained superb ideas from the free decorating service in my favorite furniture store. They also have a beautiful book called a "treasury" that is filled with color photographs of beautiful rooms. What a terrific source of ideas for room arrangement, colors, and using accessories.

The important thing to remember when you work with a decorator or furniture salesperson is that *you* are in charge. Make certain that selections are what you really want, not what the decorator thinks you should have. Decorating is a personal statement—no one should be telling you what you need or like.

# Personal taste and life-style

My story is a good illustration of the typical stages many people go through in the process of finding the right style of decorating that meshes well with their life-style. In the mid-sixties we sold our tiny, cracker-box house for a home in suburbia that was at least twice as large. The "modern" furniture we bought when we were first married was showing signs of wear, thanks to our active preschool kids. The trendy colors and skinny-armed couch and chair from 1959 were worn and dated-looking. Modern furniture changes style constantly. My taste had also changed. For our new home, I decided to buy furniture in a classic style that does not change. Then I would be happy with it forever—right? I did a pretty good job decorating that house, but I got carried away and furnished the living room and dining room in a rather formal decor. At least, it was much too fancy for our life-style. We spent our time in the family room or outdoors on the patio, and the rooms where I spent quite a few of our decorating dollars were hardly ever used.

After about six years in that house, we moved to northern California. I found a house that suited our life-style perfectly. It did not have a living room or a dining room but a combination kitchen and family room, which I decided would be one giant kitchen. What was supposed to be the living room we made into our family room. This arrangement is much the most comfortable for us.

Meanwhile, the people who bought our house with the fancy living room and dining room got those two rooms fully furnished. They were delighted, and so was I. They had two rooms already decorated in the elegant style they liked, and I was free of two museum galleries that we never used.

## Getting started

Tackling the decoration of an entire house at once is pretty daunting. Why not start with one room? When you complete one room before tackling another, you will feel that you are accomplishing something. When I say "complete one room," I mean furnish it with the basic things the room needs. You can take months or years to find the accessories and personal touches that make the room unique. Here is the help you need to get going.

- Measure the room. You may want to use graph paper and do a floor plan to scale. Mark down on the floor plan the things your room has that will not change: windows, doors, closets, etc.
- Tailor the room for its use. Ask yourself how the room will be used and who will use it. Talk to family members about your plans if they will be using the room too. Lucky for me, no one in my family cares to be involved in every decision. I get to select the wallpaper—and

to put it up. If your family members want to help make decisions, perhaps you can narrow down the selection and then involve them in the final choice.

Make a list of the things you *have,* the things you *need,* and the things you *want.* If you *have* some items in the attic or elsewhere in the house that will work well in the room, start with them. Then get the *needed* items. Take care of basics like walls, floors, window coverings, and necessary pieces of furniture so you can begin to use the room. Finally, continue on to acquire the things you *want,* a few items at a time. It is a big mistake to try to obtain everything in one shopping trip, one week, or one month.

I bought the basics for our bedroom years ago but am still adding touches. Just last year I bought a horrid-looking trunk at a flea market, which I refinished (now it's gorgeous) and use as a blanket chest. I'm still hand-piecing a blue-and-white quilt top, which is at least three years from completion. So you see, decorating can take years.

Keep measurements with you. If you come upon a terrific hall tree at a garage sale, you have the measurements of the spot where it would go in your house or apartment. I not only keep a list of such measurements in my wallet but carry a tape measure in my purse. Order free catalogs from furniture makers, kitchen equipment manufacturers, and other companies that publish idea booklets. You'll get decorating ideas from the experts at no cost.

Treat yourself to a home office, a spot that is your own private place for doing your meal planning, bill paying, account keeping, letter writing, or whatever. Where? How about a corner of the kitchen, den, family room, or bedroom? Include a desk or table, chair or stool, and adequate lighting. Take a look in stationery stores and the housewares department of variety stores for useful devices. Plastic vegetable bins that stack make great storage units. Old peanut-butter or marmalade jars hold pencils and ballpoints. On your next variety-store visit, stock up on scotch tape, paper clips, a stapler and staples, stamps, envelopes, rubber bands, and scrap paper. Having an adequately supplied office at home may save you any number of nuisance trips.

# Fill your home with color

Choose a color scheme you can live with, and use it everywhere. Be brave! Every room does not have to look the same just because you have an overall color scheme throughout your home. Blue happens to be my favorite color, and, lucky for me, my husband, Walt, likes it too. We built our color scheme around blues without a thought of which color is currently "in." If you are unsure which color you like best, start tearing out pictures of rooms you like. Visit model homes and furniture stores and note the color schemes that have the look you like.

Color can do a wonderful job of tying your entire living area together. Your rooms will seem to flow together and complement one another, instead of being chopped into rooms and hallways. The major color in one room can be used as an accent color in another room. Each room looks different, but the color scheme unifies the whole house.

- Be brave. Don't be afraid to use the colors you like. Psychologists say the easiest colors to live with are the ones found in nature.
- Select three or four colors for your basic color scheme. Then you can move accessories and furniture from room to room, and it will work with the decor.
- Light colors make things shrink back. Dark colors make things loom up large and close. If you paint a room in a light color, it will appear larger than when painted in a dark tone.
- Your eye is drawn to color. Paint or wallpaper one wall, and that wall will seem to advance. That's why I like the idea of wallpapering all four walls in a room—it makes the room seem much larger. I even wallpaper the closet doors. However, if your room is too long in one dimension, decorating one long-end wall will tend to square things off.
- Contrasting colors make things stand out. If you want a wall to look large and want the window to blend with the wall, use drapes or a shade on the window that matches or blends with the wall color. You can buy drapery fabric and wallpaper in matching designs these days.
- Color must be suited to your family in practical ways. Off-white furniture and carpeting is going to be hard to live with if you have children and pets.

- Use strong colors only in accessories so they don't overpower everything else in the room. I love the look of my twin red chairs in the living room. But I would not want a red wall, red carpeting, or a red couch.
- Get as large a sample of carpeting, wallpaper, or fabric as you possibly can and take it home to evaluate it. It is difficult to judge how fabric will look on your couch from a six-inch-square of fabric in a furniture store. When you are home, look at it in both daylight and artificial light. If you are uncertain that it is right, don't buy it. When you come upon the right one, you'll recognize it.

## WALLS—FOLLOW THE FINGERPRINTS

You don't have to repaint your hallway once a week to keep it looking good. My family can fingerprint every wall in any building in an hour or less. When I try wiping off those fingerprints, the wipe marks look almost as bad. My answer? Try something else on the walls instead of paint—especially in high traffic areas like hallways and stairways.

## Wallpaper

- My favorite wall covering is fabric-backed vinyl wallpaper. It does cost more than paint, but if it lasts a decade, it may be more cost-effective in the long run. Our hallway was papered in a flecked, off-white, fabric-backed vinyl over ten years ago, and it still looks great. Most dirt and handprints wipe right off with a damp sponge. Vinyl wallpaper is an excellent choice for any room in your home. Fabric-back vinyl is more durable than vinyl-coated paper, but if you are easily bored and a frequent redecorator, the vinyl-coated is probably better for you.

  Wallpaper comes in a mind-boggling array of styles, materials, and prices. You can buy shiny foils, flocked velvets, fancy florals, plaids, stripes and even a blue denim look paper. Narrow down your selection (that is the hard part) and bring home samples of the papers you like best. The wallpaper store personnel can tell you how to compute how much paper you need to buy. Add pizzazz to a room with wallpaper. You can hang a photographic mural, paper a ceiling, put inexpensive paper on one wall, or add a wallpaper border to painted walls.

- I'm a do-it-yourselfer when it comes to wallpaper. For beginners, the wallpaper stores have booklets with step-by-step instructions and sell kits of wallpaper tools for about $8. If you are too unsure of yourself to start that way, offer to assist a friend who knows how to wallpaper and learn by helping and watching. Unless you are doing a ceiling, wallpapering can be done by one person. However, it is always nice to have a helper. I've paid my kids to spend a Saturday helping me redo a room. We start at the crack of dawn, blast rock music on the radio, don't worry about getting paste in our hair, and work like crazy until the job is done.
- Leftover wallpaper can be used to line shelves and drawers or to paper wastebaskets or storage containers.
- Fabric-covered walls can be gorgeous. When my sister bought beautiful floral sheets for her bed, she also bought extra sheets in king size and "papered" a bedroom wall with them. A wall that matches the bed makes for really elegant sleeping. Ask in the wallpaper store about the kind of adhesive to use for applying fabric to your walls.

# Paneling

Paneling is another "forever" wall covering—expensive but permanent. Once you go to the expense of buying the materials and getting it on the wall, it is there to stay. Our living room and entry hall are paneled in off-white barnsiding paneling that was put up about ten years ago. We will never have to resurface *those* walls.

There's just the possibility, however, that its permanence may work against you. Suppose you change your mind two years from now? Or suppose you are transferred to another part of the country and must sell the house? Permanent wall covering, which the new owners would have to remove if they don't like it, could possibly make it more difficult to find a buyer.

## Paint

Painted walls cost the least and are easiest for the do-it-yourselfer. Rank beginners, even children, can use paint rollers, and it takes very little more expertise to work with a brush. Here is a tip friends of ours got from a professional painter: Outdoor paint can be used inside. It costs a bit more than indoor paint, but it lasts twice as long and is washable.

Watch for sales and buy good-quality paint. Painting is hard work and better quality paint gives a better result, is more durable and more washable. Buying cheap paint can be false economy as your project might take an additional coat of the cheaper paint. We called Sears and asked when their best quality Weatherbeater outdoor paint would be on sale again. The salesperson told us to watch for a sale to be advertised the following month. We bought it on sale and saved about one-third the cost. Then we employed our son Mike, who is a college student, to paint the house for us over semester break.

# THE FLOOR—STEP ON IT

The floor is like a stage on which the room's decor rests. Wall space is the largest area in your room and floor space is the second largest area. Take into consideration the look you like and the kind of use (or abuse) the floor will take. Then select your floor covering from the wonderful choices that are available.

## Wood floors

Wood floors can add a glowing warmth to your home. They can frame runners or area rugs beautifully. A neighbor carpeted the second story of her home to make it warmer and quieter. The first floor had wood floors and area rugs and looks beautiful. There are sealers, varnishes and waxes available that make wood floor care easy. Before buying any floor covering, find out about the care required to keep it looking good.

# Carpeting

I like wall-to-wall carpeting, even though many decorators find it to be "dreadfully boring." It is easy to zip around with the vacuum cleaner, and it makes for a warm, quiet floor covering. The wood parquet floor in our other house always looked dusty and showed wear in high traffic areas.

- Check into buying commercial or industrial carpeting. It costs more but is thick, dense, and made to wear well.
- Light carpeting will make your home seem larger than dark carpeting.
- Avoid having carpeting go right up to the door. If you step in the door onto carpeting, that area will wear and soil quickly. We put tiles that look like used brick in our entry instead of carpeting. They can be quickly mopped clean. Rubber mats and transparent plastic carpet covers are also available, but carpet manufacturers warn against putting an extra piece of floor covering on top of your carpeting. The rough backing will wear away the surface you are trying to protect. And these mats are often easy to trip over.
- You pay for every inch of your carpeting, including the scraps. Tell the carpet installer to save all the scraps. Use them
    for carpeting the back of your station wagon or car trunk
    for carpeting closet floors
    for lining a closet shelf, the bottom of a trunk, your kid's toy box, the dog's basket or house
    for a sample square to take along when you shop
    to put in the car trunk to use when you change a tire or put on snow chains
    to pad a dolly, hand truck, or other device for moving furniture

- Jiffy spot remover for carpeting/upholstery: Mix in an empty dishwashing-liquid plastic container:

    2 cups water

    1 teaspoon white vinegar

    1 teaspoon liquid dishwashing detergent

    Shake, put on clean cloth, and sponge spot from carpeting. Try not to get the carpeting very wet.

## Ceramic tile

If you're redoing a bathroom, kitchen or entry hall, you are certain to be tempted by the idea of beautiful ceramic-tile flooring. Spend your money one time, and you're set forever. But remember, ceramic tile, in addition to being expensive, can also be cold and hard to stand on for long periods. So think it over.

## Vinyl floorcovering

Like carpeting, vinyl floorcovering comes in many styles, materials and price ranges. If you are selecting a vinyl floorcovering for the heavily-used entry hall, buy something that can withstand the wear and tear. You can probably put something of lesser quality in a bathroom because it is going to get lighter wear. Shop around, ask questions, start noticing floors in other homes and ask the homeowners if they are wearing well and are easy to maintain. You might write a letter to the customer service department of a floorcovering manufacturer. Tell them the room in which you plan to install the floor, the kind of use that room gets and ask them which of their floorcoverings they recommend for your area. If anyone knows, the manufacturer certainly should. No-wax, low-sheen vinyl makes the most sense to me. High gloss floors show wear once the gloss wears off, especially in heavy traffic areas.

- You can buy remnants of vinyl flooring that are large enough to do most bathrooms. Find out what is available in your area by calling places that sell carpet remnants. Check with your floor installer as to the quantity you need before buying.

- Save vinyl flooring scraps for lining drawers and shelves. You can also tack it to the top of a workbench for a wipable surface.
- Vinyl floor tiles can usually be installed by the do-it-yourselfer. Check the home-improvement books in the library for directions or ask where you buy the tiles. My husband Walt installed vinyl tiles in our entry hall with how-to instructions from a library book.

# WINDOWS

Before spending a fortune on pleated drapes, consider the alternatives. Every window does not have to be covered. Some windows look better without heavy framing drapes or frilly, light-blocking curtains. If you intend to drape your windows, however, first telephone a dry cleaner and find out how much it will cost to clean the ones you are considering. When I did that, I decided to buy a cheaper-to-clean type.

## Valance

- Put a valance on a spring rod across the top of a window and let the sun shine in. My kitchen looks great with a valance and nothing else.
- Buy shades instead of curtains or drapes. Shades come in great-looking colors and textures. You can trim them by adding braid, fabric strips, rickrack, or ribbon—just glue it on. For a custom-made look, fabric can also be laminated to a shade with spray adhesive.
- Combine a valance with a shade or thin blinds. At night you can lower the shade for privacy and warmth. During the day it is pulled up under the valance, and no one knows it's there.

## Shutters

Inside shutters are another choice. These are not cheap, even purchased unpainted from a hardware-lumber chain and installed do-it-yourself. But they are a "forever" investment and very versatile to use. You can open both top and bottom or close top and bottom, or you can open them top only (for winter) or bottom only (for summer). Folded back at either side, they "frame" the window, too.

## Plants

- Hang a plant or two in front of a window instead of curtains or drapes. A valance across the top and a hanging plant work well together.
- Install glass shelves across a window and line them with plants. This works great on windows that open outward. You can turn an ordinary window into an attractive greenhouse with this one little trick.
- For another plant idea, here's something I once noticed in a hotel lobby and have copied and used at home. Hang a pipe from the ceiling horizontally and paint it the same color as the ceiling. The pipe should be as long as the width of the window and should be positioned about ten inches in from the panes so there is sufficient room for the plants. Now hang pots from the pipe, varying the height at which they dangle. Plants are rather heavy, so the pipe must be secured with toggle bolts or other secure fastening strong enough to support the weight.

## Curtains and drapes

- Purchase unlined fabric panels, with or without tiebacks, and curtains that can be tossed in the washer to use instead of drapes.
- Send for free mail order catalogs of curtains and then go through

them for ideas for decorating your windows—see page 54 for sources. They are chock full of illustrations for virtually any window style. You can get great ideas for sew-it-yourself curtains from these catalogs also.

- Buy drapes that do not have pleats. They can be cleaned "by the pound" in dry-cleaning machines. You can combine unpleated drapes with a shade or slim blinds.

- Sew it yourself and get a custom look for rock-bottom prices. The public library has many idea books for such sewing projects, and they are chock-full of terrific window treatments that look great and cost little. Don't be put off by the fact that a drape or curtain is large. "Large" and "difficult" are *not* synonymous. Quite the opposite, in fact, for curtains are one of the best "learning" projects.

- If you do not sew at all, pay someone to do it for you. Your neighbor may be a hotshot at the machine who could run up curtains for you in a day or two—trade her services for some specialty of yours. (See page 123.) Or call the high-school sewing teacher and ask her to advertise your project to her students or to recommend someone.

## Blinds

- Take a look at those outdoor rollup shades. They work just as well indoors and might be perfect for a window in your home.

- Don't be afraid of Brand X. I once bought some custom-made slim blinds (the kind you open and close by twisting a wand) from a mail-order house. I went to the company's retail outlet to select the color in person, then returned home and ordered them through the catalog when they were on sale. They look exactly like my friend's supercostly name-brand blinds.

# FURNISHINGS

Furniture is the most important thing you buy for your home. It has to go with your way of life. If you like to flop in a chair and put your feet up (like everyone in our family), then you had better buy pieces that are durable and practical. Some suggestions:

## Upholstery

- I prefer furniture with wood arms that are *not* covered with fabric. Soil and wear always show first on the arms of couches and chairs. You can have furniture reupholstered, but it costs almost as much as replacing the piece.
- Leather furniture costs a bundle but lasts virtually forever. Sometimes it is worth it to buy the best, because you only buy once.
- Pay extra and buy protective arm covers when you buy new upholstered furniture. They are rectangles of upholstery fabric that match your chair or couch, and they will extend the life of the piece of furniture.
- How many people usually sit on your couch? One or two, right? Buy a couch that can comfortably seat two people instead of a superlong couch that can only fit on one wall in your room. It makes for a more versatile piece of furniture, because it can be rearranged. A pair of small couches is an even better buy, because they can be set out in an L shape or face each other for a conversation area. On the other hand, if your family habitually snoozes in front of the TV, the long couch is probably more useful for you.

## Wood furniture

- Instead of buying one chair, buy a pair of matching chairs. They look good and can be arranged in many ways in your room.
- Look at used furniture. If you are willing to put in some time and elbow grease, you can refinish it yourself and have a like-new piece

of furniture. If you plan to have it professionally refinished, telephone a furniture refinisher and get a price before buying an item. That $25 chair might cost you $75 by the time it's been refinished.

- Browse in the unfinished furniture store. I was surprised at the quality and variety of furniture that is now available. You can stain or antique it yourself, and it is much easier to do than removing old finish from used furniture. Ask if other styles are available that are not shown on the showroom floor. Some stores will custom-make unfinished furniture for you. Doesn't cost a thing to ask and it is cheaper than buying finished furniture in a furniture store.

- Antiquing furniture is an easier process than refinishing. Instead of stripping the piece down to bare wood, you just paint over the finish. I once antiqued an old wooden icebox in antique red. We put shelves inside, and it is now a terrific cabinet.

- Investigate "distressed wood." Distressed wood has grooves, nicks, and marks in it when it comes from the furniture store. The furniture is supposed to be that way. I love it! When you accidentally drop your key ring on the coffee table, and it makes a new dent, you just go over the dent with scratch cover, and the new "antique marks" are covered.

- Watch flea markets and garage sales for highly usable items:
  - an extra card table or two (very handy for entertaining)
  - extra redwood picnic table (useful for potting plants or as a workbench)
  - wooden wall shelves (refinish, paint, or cover with fabric)
  - old kitchen cupboards (garage storage system)

- Director chairs can be used in any room of the house or on the patio or porch. They also fold away for easy storage. Canvas backs are replaceable and come in pow colors.

## Beds

- Need an extra bed? Buy one twin mattress and no box spring. Slide it under another bed. When one of your children has an overnight guest, slide out the mattress, cover it with a fitted sheet, and you have an instant trundle bed. If the bed is too low for the mattress to

fit under it, put the bed legs on casters or raise them on wooden blocks.
- Use a straw rug instead of a headboard. You can buy beautiful straw rugs in import stores in a variety of patterns, colors and sizes. Straw rugs are cheaper than buying a wood headboard. They add an interesting touch at low cost.

# Storage

- Make a dresser, trunk, or chest look like a cabinet or hutch by adding wall-hung shelves above it. But make sure the shelves are firmly anchored. Use toggle bolts if the wall is plaster or wall board.
- We have five trunks and could use more. Our thirty-year-old house is short on storage space, and trunks solve that problem beautifully. They are also attractive and versatile. Use a trunk for a coffee table, end table, or foot-of-bed chest. You can paint them, antique them, or leave them as they are. Glue fabric to the inside for a beautiful finishing touch. Send for a brochure or replacement parts to

> Antique Trunk Company
> 3706 West 169th Street
> Cleveland, Ohio 44111

Buy trunks
> at flea markets
> at secondhand stores or thrift shops
> at garage or yard sales
> at army surplus stores (ask for foot lockers)
> at auctions

*Note:* Trunks and chests with heavy, hinged lids should *not* be used by young children as toy chests. They often "hide" inside and get imprisoned, sometimes suffocating. Heavy lids can come down accidentally, causing injury to children.

*Idea:* Put a cedar slat liner on the floor of the trunk. Cedar slats are tongue-in-groove and easy to install. Looks good, smells good!

- An el cheapo book case can be made decorative by the use of fancy cinder block and cork board—a variation on the old bricks-and-boards concept so popular with college students. This idea was, in fact, supplied by my college-age son Steve.

# Plants

Special touches make your home unique. Plants are my favorite accessory—they add a special touch to every room of the house.

- Go to a nursery to look at houseplants and to get your questions answered. Then jot down the names of the kinds of plants you want and buy them at a discount store.

   *Caution:* Use discount stores for small houseplants *only*. Buy large expensive ones at nurseries, where you will be assured of a healthy, well-cared for plant, whose seller will stand behind his product.

- Inexpensive clay flowerpots with a drainage hole in the bottom are the best. Their porous sides allow the plant to "breathe." You can buy matching saucers, too, but personally, although I dislike plastic pots, I prefer plastic saucers to clay ones, because they do not sweat. Buy them in clay color to match the pots. Put a small rock or shard over the drainage hole so it can lose water without losing planting soil.

- Plant small plants around the base of a tall one for a supergreen look.

- Group plants. Three or four plants look better in a group than when separate. But if you have several of contrasting look but similar soil and watering needs, plant them all in one large pot. Otherwise, make a grouping from several separate pots.

- Make a room divider with plants. Hang them at different levels from a ceiling pole.

- Ceramic tiles are perfect for placing under plants. Tile stores have them in virtually every size and color. I lined our bathroom windowsills with tiles to make a plant-proof surface (the damp air of bathrooms is good for plants, by the way). Glue felt on the back of the tiles if you intend to place them on a wooden table top—their undersurfaces are rough and scratchy.

- Buy plants in small sizes—they are cheaper and more fun to watch grow. Feed them plant food and don't overwater. Make sure they have adequate sun or artificial light. Transplant to larger pots only when they get potbound, for if you give roots too much room, all the plant's growing energy will go there instead of into the leaves.

- If you're experienced with house plants, propagate them with rooting powder in water or damp sand. Ask your neighbor for cuttings from her plants, too, if she has some you particularly admire.

- Sick plants. If I suspect that one of my small plants is diseased or infested with a creepy crawler, I trash it. Insecticides don't always work and are dangerous to use and costly, so I'd rather throw away a cheap plant, including the dirt in the flowerpot. However, big, expensive, decorative plants are worth trying to save. Consult the nursery where you bought them. The nurseryman can recommend the right insecticide, advise you how to improve your watering, feeding, and misting practices—and possibly even tell you that the plant is just going through a normal phase. Or if you are near a horticultural society or botanical garden, check to see if they have a consultation service—many do.

- Put your plants in interesting containers and place them in original positions. Baskets are perfect for holding plants. Plants also look great when sitting on the top of a high piece of furniture and trailing down the side. I use some old scales to hold plants, and I love the way they look.

# Wall hangings

Blank walls are boring. Grab a hammer and nails and get something up there.

- Stretched fabric can be instant pizzazz for a dead wall. Go to a fabric store and buy a fabric picture. Some stores sell a packaged combination—fabric panel plus four stretchers. Just tack the stretchers together and staple on the fabric. Or you can go to an art store and buy the stretchers and attach any fabric you choose.

- Make a family portrait gallery. Have prints enlarged to fit ready-made frames, and hang your collection on the wall for everyone to enjoy.

- Do-it-yourself framing. Do-it-yourself frame shops sell the materials and have the tools, equipment and work area available for your use. The stores in our area provide how-to instructions and have a helper available if you are all thumbs. When my husband, Walt, made frames for a grouping of old interesting documents we bought at a flea market, he needed help making the first frame. After that, he could produce the other half dozen on his own. It was much cheaper than having the framing done at a frame shop. Some experienced "framers" buy used frames at garage sales and flea markets and then cut them down to size for their framing needs.

  If you are not sure which frame will best suit your item to be framed, ask for advice at the do-it-yourself frame shops. Or go to a regular frame shop and look at some of their samples.

- When grouping pictures or objects on a wall, define the area you wish to cover, and then group the objects within that space. Make a scale drawing on paper first if you are unsure how you want your wall to look. Start with a background area ruled off to the wall's dimensions (1 inch to 1 foot is the usual scale). Then make and cut out to the same scale squares, rectangles, ovals, and so on to represent the decorations you are planning to hang. You can then move them around until you find the arrangement you like best—before you nail the first picture hanger into your wall. For example:

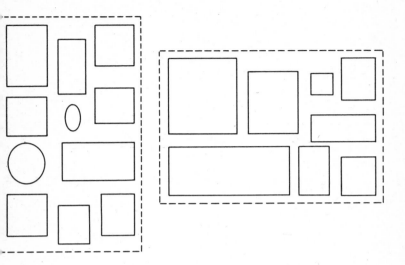

- Posters, maps, and art prints make great wall art, and you can often get them at rock-bottom prices.
- Magazine covers make excellent wall art also. At a used-book sale I once bought four old *New Yorker* magazines from the 1950s. I chose four that had interesting covers, framed them in ready-made 8" × 10" dime-store frames, and hung them up as a grouping. They look fabulous. The magazines cost 10¢ each, and the frames with glass came to $2.50 each. So for about $11 I had a set of four terrific pictures.
- Buy original art at student art shows. Check with your high school or college to find out if they hold annual sales. You will be pleasantly surprised at the quality of students' work. I've seen sculpture, pottery, weavings, and wall hangings that could be sold in very fine stores.
- Use strips of mirror attached to wall instead of solid mirror. You'll get the same space-expanding illusion at much lower cost.

- Look for low-cost and handsome antique frames at thrift shops and auctions and frame a mirror for your entrance way or over the mantel. Cheaper than artwork and very effective.

## Accessories

- Baskets with tops make great affordable storage places. In fact, low-cost baskets are the budget decorator's best friend. Hang them on the wall, group them in the kitchen or living room as organizers, and use them to hold appealing dried flower arrangements. I bought a big bunch of dried baby's breath which I stuck in a round basket and when this permanent bouquet gets dusty, I just dust it off with my hair dryer.

- If you collect seashells or rocks or almost anything, don't keep your treasures in drawers or boxes; get them out and incorporate them with your decor. Make a rock arrangement in a what-not. Display your matchbook collection as you would a set of photographs. Arrange your seashells or whatever in an interesting and attractive pattern on your wall. Use your imagination, and if you are unsure of how to show the items off to best advantage, consult an artistic friend.

- Quaint, out-of-date items (kitchen utensils, woodworking tools, and so forth) often make charming wall displays. Ask any family "collector" if he or she has any of these old-fashioned items that you may have. My mother had squirreled away a bunch of old kitchen gadgets and a carpet beater, which now look great on our kitchen walls. She also had a pile of cross-stitched samplers she had never gotten around to framing. My sister, daughter, and I went through the samplers, and each chose one to frame. Mother also had two old dolls that were in distressed condition, at best. I whisked them off to a doll hospital and had them cleaned, repaired, and dressed. The cost for fixing up the two dolls was about $60, but they are now worth much more. (I could have saved some of that money by dressing the dolls myself—a fun kind of sewing and a good way to use up fabric ends.) Find out if there are any oldies but goodies in boxes, attics, or drawers that will add interest and pleasure to the decor in your home.

*Special Ideas Department:* It is the special individual touches that make an apartment or house uniquely yours. Often these imaginative ideas and methods can be added at little or no cost.

- Put shelves or bookcases under a staircase to capture lost space.
- Put a shelf in your laundry room above the washer and dryer. Have a deep dishpan, basket, or box for each family member. When clothes come out of the dryer you can sort them immediately into the containers. Family members must collect their laundry and return containers to the shelf. Sure speeds up sorting out laundry and cuts down on the cries of "Where's my sweatshirt?"

# Sheets

- When you're in the market for sheets and towels, buy "seconds." The flaws are virtually invisible, and you will save considerably.
- Designer sheets usually cost a lot. If you fall in love with linens you simply can't afford, buy the pillowcases only, and then buy no-name sheets in a plain color to go with them. You could also splurge on one flat sheet in a "designer" print. Cut that sheet into strips to use to add a touch of elegance to plain sheets. Add bands of color along the hems for a terrific look at low cost. You can get a lot of mileage out of one print sheet!
- Buy sheets in a different color for each bedroom. If your linen closet is small, store sheets and pillowcases on a closet shelf in the bedroom where they are used.
- Sew braid or eyelet to plain sheets and pillowcases for a low-budget, elegant look. Works great for towels too. Decorated linens make great gifts too.
- Sheets can work decorative magic. Buy an extra sheet or two to match your linens and use it in imaginative ways.

    Staple or glue it to a wall.

    Line a trunk.

    Make a tablecloth.

    Make a dust ruffle for your bed.

    Make decorative pillows (check pattern books for easy-to-make pillow patterns).

    Cover a window shade.

Glue strips of fabric on a shade to decorate.
Sew strips to curtains or drapes.
Cover a chair cushion.
Make tiebacks for curtains or drapes.
Glue or tack onto wooden shelves (paint brackets in coordinating color).
Make a runner for table or dresser.
Make curtains.
Make a "skirt" for your old bathroom sink.
Glue onto cardboard boxes to make containers to hold magazines, etc.

# Bring the outdoors in

Look out the windows or glass doors in your home. Is there something you can add to the outside that will enhance the room inside.

- Place a bird feeder or bird bath outside a window that can be seen from your favorite chair. Keep the binoculars handy.
- Hang a blooming plant. We have a moss-packed wire basket filled with fuschias hanging right outside the kitchen window. Most attractive. Remember, though, that the blooming season soon ends.
- Sliding glass doors provide a view of the outside. We put some redwood posts and a few cross beams from which we hang plants. It has a gazebo or green house effect. In the hot summer, we unroll inexpensive wooden slat blinds across the top to shade the sliding doors from the afternoon sun. It is pretty and practical and an inviting place to step outdoors and sit in the shade.

# Scrounging

Take advantage of other people's usable discards. Scrounging may make you feel sheepish at first, but this quickly passes—especially once you discover how many of your friends are doing the same thing.

- University dump sites are a great place to look, especially at the end of the school year. My daughter, who is attending summer school this year, discovered that the students who were going home for the holidays piled all the stuff they could not carry off into their dormitory or apartment-house trash bins. She drove from dumpster to dumpster and picked up two card-table chairs, a plastic laundry basket, a parched Boston fern, and a couch. The couch was the ugliest shade of army green you will ever see, but she enlisted help in carrying it to her apartment and covered it with a floral-print bed sheet, and it looks fine. When she graduates, she will put it back by the dumpster for the next scrounger.

- Keep an eye peeled for curbside discards. Some years ago, a couple I know of, expecting their first baby, came across a discarded crib. The husband was still in graduate school then, and they were broke, so they hauled the crib home, washed it, painted it, and used it for the baby—and all his subsequent nine siblings. By then the father was a senior civil servant and doing well, but they had grown too fond of the crib to part with it.

- Try doctors' row or a medical-arts building if there is one near you—the tonier the better. Doctors, especially the high-priced variety, frequently redecorate their waiting rooms, and the rejects are often of excellent quality and in excellent shape.

## Cleaning

- Everyone enjoys a clean, attractive home. Who is responsible for the never-ending chore of picking up? All the people who live there—wherever "there" is. The entire family should pitch in to keep it neat and clean.

- The cleanup team consists of all members of the household working together until the job is done. Set aside a specific amount of time and have the cleanup scheduled on a regular basis. Maybe you can put a casserole in the oven late Sunday afternoons and then schedule the cleanup from 4:30 until 6 P.M. Or, if Sunday is too unconventional a cleaning day, pencil in Saturday morning—before the ball game and after the Friday night date. Pick the day and the time that best suits the most members of the group and stick to that schedule.

- Touch-ups. In between cleanups, take a few minutes to do quickie touch-ups, such as wiping up the bathroom sink, the top of the stove, or the counter tops. You can accomplish these while the dinner cooks or before you leave for work, or a child can take over a certain chore—dust-mopping under beds, say—every Wednesday after school (or whatever).
- Spring cleaning. Most houses need a major behind-the-ears turning out once a year or so. Forget about pulling the whole house apart at once. List all the tasks that have to be done, and then tackle them one by one. Do one room at a time and clean it thoroughly and systematically, taking as many days for this as you need. Then proceed to the next room, and so on, until the deep cleaning is done.
- Divide big jobs into little pieces. Instead of spending a big chunk of time cleaning one thing, divide the job up into five segments. Put in one hour per day of cleaning time during the week and take Saturdays and Sundays off from housework.
- Hire help for the heavy work. Hire one of your children or a neighborhood high-school student to do major cleaning (or minor if you need it) for you.

# 4

# SUPER EASY LOW-COST ENTERTAINING

Entertaining can be a great success when you do it the easy way. Gourmet foods and formal elegance have little or nothing to do with putting on a successful get-together. What makes entertaining a true success is a relaxed host/hostess and the right group of people. Here are some secrets.

79

# PLANNING

Careful planning—and starting early—is the key to success when it comes to most forms of entertaining. Choose people you like, some tasty food, delicious drinks, then relax and enjoy yourself. A relaxed and friendly atmosphere is essential for a happy party.

## Guests

Jot down a list of the people you plan to invite. You can gather together a group of people who have common occupations or interests so conversation will be very easy. Or you can deliberately put together a diverse group of people. When you do this, the host and/or hostess must be sure that the group mixes well and no one is left standing on their own.

- To stop your guests from sitting or standing in one spot for the entire party, place food and drinks in several locations in the room. Then there is a reason to go to more than one spot. It is a good way to get the groups to mix and mingle. If someone doesn't want to mix, there is nothing you can do—one couple we know always heads for the couch and sits there for the entire evening like a pair of bookends—but you can make it easy for those who do wish to move around and meet people.
- Make it a rule that guests may *not* sit with their spouses at dinner, so people will begin conversations with others.
- Another setup that makes for nice conversation groups is to assign people to different dinner tables (use four card tables, seating four people each, instead of one long table with places for sixteen). You can use place cards or give people numbers that match the number on the table where they will eat. Make certain you don't have two members of the same couple or family or two best friends at the same table. Someone who wants to spend the evening glued to his best friend or spouse can do that before or after dinner.

- Tell your guests how to dress. If the party is supercasual or a rather dressy, formal affair, say so. With young guests, specify whether or not they are to wear shoes.
- Keep a record of guests' preferences. In a small notebook, jot down the date, guest list, menu, and drinks served. Keep track of what your guests prefer to drink, which dish went over like a house afire, and which went uneaten, the outfits you wore when and in front of whom, which people formed a whiz-bang group and which didn't, and so on. Next time, if the same group of people is coming, and you want to serve them something different from last time, check your entertainment log to find out what you served. If your party was such a smash that you intend to invite the same group again, your log will tell you who they were. On the other hand, if your party sank like a stone, a notebook will help you to determine why, so you can avoid errors in the future.

## Preparations

- Plan your party from A to Z. Plan the menu carefully and make certain you have everything you need. Think the whole party through carefully beforehand. Then you won't have to dash out frantically at the last moment to shop for forgotten items.
- Set up the bar for self-service. Free yourself from being bartender for the evening. Mix the first drink for each guest and then allow guests to serve themselves.
- Provide nonalcoholic beverages for guests who do not drink.
- Chill punch without diluting it by freezing one of the punch ingredients (like orange juice) in a large bowl or mold. It will melt slowly and keep the punch cold. Or you can float a Baggie filled with ice cubes that is fastened shut. The cubes melt inside the bag and do not dilute the punch. Fish it out before the guests arrive.
- For tidbits with drinks, serve seasonal fresh vegetables, crisp whole grain crackers with cheese, ethnic specialties (check Mexican, Middle Eastern, Scandinavian cookbooks).
- Have your own salad bar. At buffet dinners, serve the salad course

---

### Battle Plan

**6:30**  *drinks/hors d'oeuvres*

**6:45**  *oven 350—Put chicken dish in oven;
dinner in 45 min.*

**7:00**  *mix salad
pour water/wine?*

**7:30 ish**  *Serve dinner
Plug in coffee
Tea—ask?*

**7:45**  *Dessert from freezer*

**8:00**  *Serve dessert
coffee*

---

salad-bar style. Let guests fix their own salads from bowls of ingredients and a variety of dressings.

- Make sure food looks as good as it tastes. Add attractive little touches that cost little or nothing: a thin lemon slice in water glasses at dinner; a paper doily between the coffee cup and saucer; a bright green sprig of parsley or watercress on each plate. Copy ideas from restaurants. Little touches add a lot.

# On the night

- Make introductions easy. When you have a large group of people, do not try to introduce all the guests to one another. As each guest arrives, take him to a small group and introduce him to that group. After that, he's on his own.

  Make sure you introduce him the way he prefers. Some people resent being addressed by their first names by total strangers. Others are chilled by formal last names or find them too difficult to learn or object to having to spell out their own, and prefer to settle for first names or even nicknames. Introductions should be made as untraumatic as possible for all concerned.

- Stick to your schedule. Serve dinner at whatever time you said you would. Your guests are probably hungry and were mentally planning to eat at that time. Moreover, when you extend cocktail time, you spend more on liquor.

- Keep an eye out during the evening for people who may be having difficulty mixing. Make sure every guest is having a good time by bringing loners up to a group and introducing him/her. It may be difficult for a shy person to walk up to a stranger and begin a conversation but if you provide a little information and some warmth, conversation can easily get under way.

## The easiest parties in the world

Entertaining is extra easy and fun when you don't have to do all the work and incur all the expenses. Here are some of my favorite ideas for joint entertaining. They'll allow you to entertain more often *and* have more fun.

- **Summertime Barbecue and/or Swim Party.** The host/hostess supplies paper plates, utensils, charcoal grill(s) for barbecuing, and beverages. (Instead of costly canned beverages, I make a vat of iced tea or lemonade.) Guests bring meat for their families to grill on the barbecue (hot dogs, burgers, steak, whatever), plus a salad, vegetable, or dessert to share. Borrow extra barbecue grills from friends and neighbors if you need to, and have tongs and potholder mitts handy.

---

*Summer Sunday Swim Session*
*Dinner too!*

*Bring: swimsuits & towel*
       *meat for your family to barbeque*
       *big salad to share that*
       *serves 10*

*We'll have beverages, plates & utensils,*
*barbeque supplies, pool, sunshine and a*
*fun group of people.*

*Sunday, Aug. 8*              *Call if*
*2:30 pm (Dinner at 5)*  *you can't*
                              *come!*
                              *123-4567*

---

- **Picnic at the Park (or Beach).** Pick a day and time and invite everyone to meet you at the park or beach. Bring along equipment for softball or volleyball, or frisbees to toss.

---

*Join us at Capitola Beach!*
*Sat. July 11th 1:30 ish*

*Bring picnic supper*
       *beach blanket*
       *frisbee, . . .*

*We'll be by Lifeguard Stand #3*

*The Schaffers*

---

**Your Basic Pot Luck.** You prepare the main course and ask others to bring salads, desserts, hors d'oeuvres. I let my guests know what the main course will be so they can bring food that complements it.

---

*Join in—good food, fun people, too!*

*Call Barbara Jean*
*if you can't come!*

*I'm making Lasagne for everyone.*

*Please bring* _____ *to*
*serve* _____ .

*Friday, May 4th, 7 pm*
*Regrets only!   (Dinner at 8 pm)*

---

**Sinful Dessert Party** (my favorite kind of gathering). You make coffee, tea, and punch. Ask each guest or couple to bring their favorite dessert to share. For this evening, calories don't count.

---

*Sinful Dessert Party*

*8 pm Sat. Sept. 21st*
*(Call if you can't come!)*

*Bring your favorite dessert*
*to share . . . calories don't*
*count.*

*Barbara Jean*

---

- **Special Event Party (World Series, Super Bowl, Whatever).** Invite a large crowd, serve pretzels and popcorn, beer and wine. Make a chart for placing bets on the game, with winners the end of each quarter. If you invite a huge group of people, photocopy the invitation.

---

*Annual Super Bowl Party*
*Sunday, Jan. 21st*

| | | |
|---|---|---|
| *Pregame Fun* | *1:30 pm* | *Place your lucky bets.* |
| *Kick off* | *2:15 pm* | *Casual Dress!* |

*Football, food & friends!*

*Please come . . .*    *Barbara Jean*

---

- **Progressive Dinners—outdoors or in.** Plan a progressive dinner with friends or neighbors. All participants host a portion of the party. Hors d'oeuvres and cocktails are served in one location

---

*Progressive Dinner—Sat. June 11*

| | | |
|---|---|---|
| *Cocktails & hors d'oeuvres* | *6:30* | *Judy & Joe* |
| *Salad* | *7:15* | *Beth & Phil* |
| *Entree* | *8:00* | *Barbara & Walt Gloria & Martel* |
| *Dessert & Coffee* | | *at Barb & Elmer's* |

---

(it can be BYOB, Bring Your Own Bottle), then the group moves on to the next location for the salad course. The main course is served in a third location. You can have two couples host the main course, since this is usually more expensive and more work than the other parts of the meal. Dessert and coffee/tea are served in the last party place for the evening. Not only is the cost and work shared over the group, but moving from place to place helps your group mix around. Progressive dinners can be held outdoors in good weather and the main course can be a barbecue.

**Instant Cocktail Party.** Everyone brings a munchie to share and his own bottle. The host/hostess provides ice and mixers. The host can also provide coffee/tea and wine.

---

*Party to celebrate Sue's birthday (39th—again!)*

*BYOB and a munchy to share.*   •

*8 pm Sat. March 14th at Joe's*

---

**Before the Big Event Party.** Invite a group over for a glass of wine and hors d'oeuvres before going to a show, or party, or out to dinner. It is less expensive and much more intimate than sitting in a bar, a nice way to begin an evening.

> *Join us for a glass of*
> *wine before showtime!*
>
> *7:00 Feb. 11th*
> *before "Annie"*
>
> *Hope you can come—*
> *Barbara Jean*

- **To-Live-Is-to-Eat-Chocolate Party.** Invite chocoholic friends
  indulge in an evening of chocolate eating. Ask everyone to brin♭
  chocolate dessert. Serve a special chocolate-flavored coffee. B
  napkins in a nice, chocolate brown. You might ask everyone for h
  recipe and compile a chocolate cookbook. Or ask everyone to ♭
  the recipe beside the dessert dish and provide blank cards ♭
  anyone who wants to jot these down.

> *Attention all Chocolate lovers!!!*
>
> *Important evening meeting at*
> *Barbara Jean's: 8 pm Sun. Nov. 5th*
>
> *Agenda:   Sample all chocolate*
> *desserts.*
>
> *Bring:   Your favorite chocolate*
> *dessert and the recipe.*

**Super Salad Bar Luncheon.** Set up a salad bar—bowls of greens, onions, olives, radishes, cucumbers, beets, beans, sprouts, bacon bits, croutons, and other salad munchies. Provide a variety of dressings. Corn or bran muffins or bread sticks plus the salad bar make a wonderful do-it-yourself luncheon.

---

*Super Salad Luncheon*

*noon, Friday, Aug. 16th*
*at Barbara Jean's*

*Call if you can't come!*
*B.J.*

---

**Calling All "Grape Nuts."** Wine and cheese parties are enjoyable and easy to host. You supply the cheese and crackers and wine-glasses. Guests bring a bottle of their favorite wine to place on the wine-tasting table (so what if two are the same?). Get a few books on wine from the library and put them on the table too. If grapes are in season, buy a few bunches for a beautiful, edible centerpiece.

---

*Calling all "grape nuts"*

*Wine-tasting get-together*

*Fri. May 5th 7:30*

*Bring a bottle of your favorite wine to put on the tasting table.*
   *Come and enjoy—*
     *B.J.*

- **Another Wine and Cheese Gathering.** Ask each guest couple to bring a bottle of wine with the label removed. They mu put a sticker on their bottle of wine and give it a number between and 100, which is reported to the host. Guests sample wines and j down the identification number on the bottle and tell what kind wine they think it is. The person who identifies the most wine correctly is the winner. The prize, provided by the host, is a bott of wine (of course!).

- **Cookie Swap Party.** Now here is a delicious party idea. This is perfect party idea for the holiday time. Each guest brings thre dozen cookies and takes home an assortment of three doze cookies. This party can be held in the afternoon or evening. Invi six guests and ask each guest to bring three dozen cookies (the should use their favorite recipe for a special holiday cookie) bagge in six packages of half a dozen cookies each. Ask the guests to put label on each Baggie of cookies or a slip of paper inside telling th name of the cookie and the name of the person who did the bakin Cookie bags are put on a big table and each guest gets to take on Baggie from each pile except the cookies they brought. You home with six half dozen packages of cookies and everyone els gets a sample package of the cookies you brought to share. Yo might compile a recipe collection from the cookie recipes and gi everyone a copy when you have it compiled.

*Come to the Cookie Swap!*
*Sunday, Dec. 21 at 2 pm*
*at Barbara Jean's*

*Bring 3 dozen of your favorite*
*holiday cookies & the recipe.*
*Bag the cookies in 6 bags of*
*6 cookies each. Label each bag*
*with the cookie name & your name.*

*Regrets only—555-1236*

- **Tree Trimming Party.** Put up the tree and invite family and/or friends to help hang the ornaments. Serve a bowl of dairy eggnog and some hot mulled cider. My favorite recipe for hot mulled cider is equal parts of orange juice and apple cider. I use about 6 or 8 cups of each. Add one half cup of brown sugar, and 5 whole cloves, 5 whole allspice and 4 cinnamon sticks. If you don't have whole spices, you can just sprinkle in some ground spices instead. Heat and serve hot. I put it in the crock pot with a ladle; guests can serve themselves.

> *Tis the season to trim the tree!*
>
> *Please join the tree trimming fun at the Grubers'*
>
> *7:30 ish*
> *Dec. 19th*
>
> *Cider, eggnog & popcorn will be served.*

- **Special Broadcast Party.** Invite friends or relatives over to join you in watching something special that will be shown on television. It might be a special holiday concert, ballet, movie or sports event. Pop a bowl of popcorn, make a pot of coffee and a pitcher of punch, turn on the television and you're all set for a pleasant evening.

> *Join us to make a TV*
> *special even more special . . .*
>
> *Tues. Dec. 19th*
> *8 pm*
> *The Nutcracker Ballet*
>
> *The Grubers*
>
> *Hope you can come!*

## HELPFUL HINTS

# Equipment for entertaining

Do you postpone entertaining because you don't have all the necessary equipment and dread the after-entertaining clean up? Your problems will be solved by reading my hints for equipment and cleanup.

- Buy pieces that can be used for many purposes. A glass punch bowl can be a supersize salad bowl.

- Rectangular glass pans like those in your cupboard can be used for serving hors d'oeuvres. Place a bowl in the middle of the dish to hold the dip or spread and put the whole thing in a basket made to hold that size of glass pan.
- Buy shells in an import store that can be used for baking. I have baked individual clam appetizers in the shells and have used them as artichoke dishes. They are not expensive and come in a package. These are real seashells, and believe it or not, you can put them in the dishwasher.
- Share ownership in some gear used for entertaining. Get together with a friend or relative on a thirty-cup percolator. Ours cost less than $20 at a discount store and comes in very handy about three or four times a year. My neighbor and I co-own it, and she keeps it in her closet. Neither of us uses it enough to warrant having one of our own. Other items that are terrific to co-own:
  - warming trays
  - punch bowls
  - chafing dishes
  - meat slicers
  - huge trays

  Talk to neighbors and friends about sharing items that are not used everyday.
- Buy an extra card table or two. These come in very handy for entertaining. You can make inexpensive tableclothes from yardage or sheets. Watch garage sales and flea markets for extra tables.
- Use your camping or portable ice chest like a giant ice bucket. Fill it with ice, beer, sodas, and wine, and keep it all cold for a large group of people.
- Fill the washing machine with ice and use it as a giant ice bucket. When you need to refill the portable ice chest, get more cold drinks from the washing machine. Then you don't have to cram your refrigerator with cold drinks. When you are done, remove ice chunks and drinks and spin out the leftover water.
- Stop feeling guilty for not using fancy crystal and glass. I had lovely sets of both that I virtually never used, since it did not suit our

casual, informal style of entertaining. So I sold it all. If you feel the same way, advertise your sets in the paper, and you can probably sell them for at least what you paid. Or retire the elegant set to glass-doored cabinets for display and replace it with reasonably priced, attractive dishes and glassware you can enjoy without living in fear of chipping a piece.

- Keep blocks of ice on hand and bags of cubes. Whenever you finish a carton of milk, fill the rinsed carton with water and put it in the freezer. Then you will have block ice handy when you need it. Keep an extra bagful of cubes too.

## Clean up

- To lighten cleanup chores, fill a big bowl with hot, sudsy water for utensils and a dishpan for dishes and pans. As you clear the table, put dishes and utensils in to soak. Hours later, when it is time to clean up, the job will be much easier.
- For outdoor barbecues with disposable plates, have everyone bus his own dishes. This almost eliminates cleanup.
- Pay your teenager or a neighborhood teen to be a "cleaner-upper" for your party. They will usually be happy to earn the money and you enjoy your party a whole lot more.

# 5

# GOING PLACES AND DOING THINGS

It is possible to keep down the cost of having fun. All it takes is a bit of planning and knowing the type of recreation or vacation that suits you best. How do you like to spend your leisure time?

> tightly scheduled?
> completely unscheduled?
> a balanced mixture of scheduled and unplanned?

Some people like vacations so highly scheduled that they preplan activities for every waking moment. Others like a trip that allows them to do things when the spirit moves them. To have a successful vacation or other recreational activity, you have to know yourself, so that you can do things *you* most enjoy.

## Vacation Trips

Start reading the travel section of your local newspaper or the vacation ideas in the magazines you read. Sometimes we narrow our horizons because we don't know about bargain rates or low-cost tours or off-season adventures. So the next time you're near a travel agent, ask about budget tours. And the next time you're at the library, look for guides to places you've always dreamed about. Take advantage of all the free advice you can find, and you'll find yourself having the best vacations you've had in years—and at remarkable savings.

- Start a vacation ideas file or envelope. Clip and save articles from magazines and newspapers about day trips and vacation spots that look interesting. Review your file when you start thinking about your "getaway."
- Ask people who've been there. If friends and relatives have taken a trip that sounded interesting, talk to them. Find out what they liked and disliked, what they would change if they went back to that place again. You can profit by the information even if your trip is arranged quite differently from theirs.
- Remember that flying isn't the only way to go, even if you are traveling across country. Check into the cost and availability of bus or train service. It will probably be much cheaper, and it may even be more convenient or faster. And you'll see more en route.
- Tailor your travel plans to suit yourself. Our friends were amazed that we missed seeing so many tourist sights in Hawaii. But as far as we were concerned, we did not "miss" anything—we spent our time on the beaches. Riding in the car, standing in lines, and going to tourist-type places is not our idea of a vacation. But if beaches

bore you silly and you'd rather see historical sites, botanical gardens, art and crafts exhibits, and tourist attractions in general then do plan your trip around sightseeing.

- Why not plan a vacation with out-of-town friends or family members by meeting at an appealing spot located geographically between you? It can be very enjoyable to see people this way because no one has to play host and everybody gets to relax more. A good way to vacation and visit at the same time.
- Attend a summer course or seminar related to your employment. You can take an income-tax deduction for that portion of the trip that relates to the course: travel, food, lodging, and tuition. Last summer in Portland, Oregon, I taught a course for educators, to which teachers came from all over the United States and even from a few foreign countries. They enjoyed themselves, learned-something, and were able to deduct many expenses. Check with your tax adviser, however, before you sign up for a summer, job-related course.
- Many resorts have different rates for high, middle, and low seasons. Schedule your trip for the middle season, immediately before or after the high season. You can just about count on good weather. But unless your vacation is to be an indoor one, be on guard about going at the cheapest, low-season time. You run the risk of bad weather, which can ruin your vacation and make it not worth the money you save.

## On the way

- Attention all bargain hunters! Dash to a bookstore in the vacation area (or look in the airport bookstore) for a bargain-hunter's shopping guide. Then you can hit the spots not usually known to tourists.
- Don't feel obligated to bring back armloads of gifts for friends and relatives from your travels. Instead, invite them over for dessert to share your experiences. You can show your best slides or pictures—just the best ones, not all 101. They will certainly enjoy that

more than getting an ashtray emblazoned with "I Left My Heart in Alcatraz."

- Find out about low-cost fun in advance. Write or call the chamber of commerce in the area you plan to visit, or write to the state department of tourism in the state capital (that may not be the literal name for the office, but your letter will reach the right place, never fear). Request free literature and a map and specify information about low-cost activities—parks, museums, restored homes, art galleries, and so on. You'll probably receive a package of brochures two inches thick.

- Be open-minded. Enjoy what you are doing at the time and avoid comparisons with other vacations you have taken. You don't have to go to the Greek Islands or Japan to have fun. Enjoy close-to-home vacations to the fullest.

- When you're going the low-cost way, take minor irritations and inconveniences in stride. Think of new experiences as an adventure. If you expect all the comforts of home, you'll be too upset by trivial mishaps to enjoy yourself. *Expect* little things to go wrong.

- Keep a little notebook for tidbits of information that relate to traveling. If you like a certain motel or hotel or a particular campsite in Yosemite, jot it down. Then you can go there when you return or recommend it to friends. If you don't like your accommodations, warn yourself and friends off. The same for restaurants, second-hand bookstores, flea markets, farmers' markets, and so on. Preserve the addresses of "finds" that are located down side streets or on back roads so you can locate them again.

- Make certain the souvenirs you purchase in your travels are either really unique or really inexpensive. The winery near me gives tours and sells wine in its gift shop. But you can buy the same wine at the same price anywhere in the United States, so why bother? It is fun to shop, but remember, you do have to lug the things around with you.

# FUN CLOSE TO HOME

## Day trips

- Take advantage of sunny weather, and bike, hike, or picnic at your local public park. Your tax dollars provide for facilities in your area—are you using them?
- Buy a book at a local bookstore (or borrow it from the local library) about attractions and historical sites in your immediate area. Then make a day of it.
- Arrange a series of day trips. The secret to this is to plan the outing, write it in ink on the calendar, and then *go!* Don't end up painting the bathroom instead. Visit the zoo or museum, take the kids to an amusement park, tour a shopping center you've never been to before, and so on.
- Get a map of the public transportation system in your area. You'll be amazed at all the places you can get to at low cost. Collect a group of fun friends and make it an adventure.
- Treat yourself to a bus ride—a day in a nearby city or a day tour in the countryside. Call the scheduling information number for the major bus companies in your area to see what is available. Riding the bus is relatively economical, and you can read, people-watch, or snooze as you travel.

  A word to the wise, however: Bus stations can be gathering places for unsavory characters, so think twice before using the public rest rooms (take a peek to see how the place looks) and try not to arrive or leave late at night.

## Programs and special outings

- Question your public librarian to find out if there are special programs for adults or children coming up soon. Then make a family outing.
- Purchase an inexpensive pup tent to set up in your backyard, if it is safe to do so in your area. Check the prices at the military surplus store. Then allow your children to "camp out" at home.

- Be on the lookout for special discounts at attractions in your area. Grocery or department stores occasionally offer discount tickets to local events.
- Or perhaps you or your husband gets discount cards at work. My husband does, and we use them to attend many local attractions. They add up to quite a saving.
- Do movie theaters in your area have a "twilight" show, starting about five o'clock? Often these early shows carry sharply reduced prices, and they let out early enough that you can attend on a school night without earning the wrath of your babysitter's parents.
- Schools and colleges nearly always sponsor shows and concerts by their students and/or guest performers, which are quite low-cost. Get your name on the mailing list of the school near you or call the office and find out what's planned for the upcoming season. You will be impressed with the quality of amateur performances, and you will love the ticket prices.
- Buy a children's wading pool with rigid sides—mine was $12 at a discount house. Fill it with water, allow the sun to solar-heat the pool while you are hunting up a good book or stack of magazines you've been wanting to read. Fix yourself a cool drink and climb into your "spa." If the day is too hot for a warm-water soak, then set it up in the shade—or in front of the TV in your apartment living room.

  I treat myself to forty-five minutes in my "spa" daily. No kiddies allowed. I put a long cord on the telephone and set it right beside the pool. At the end of summer, we store the pool on the rafters in our garage.
- Pick up the telephone and dial local museums and art galleries to find out about special programs, courses, or tours you might enjoy. Don't wait for summer. Winters are the best seasons for indoor treats.
- Make a local-activities file. Read your city newspaper carefully. Clip and save articles about upcoming events and places you want to visit. Mark down don't-miss items on your most prominent calendar, so the dates won't slip past you unnoticed.
- Find a budget health club. Local departments of recreation, commu-

nity colleges, YMCAs, and senior-citizens centers often offer exercise classes and sports programs at supercheap rates. Get on their mailing lists. Our community college offers exercise classes, dance classes, instruction in lifetime sports like tennis, golf, and swimming. Find out when events calendars and course schedules are mailed. Jot it down on your calendar, so you can call them if you do not receive one.

- Take an academic or skills course. Local high schools and community colleges—and state and private universities, too—offer many extension-division night courses for adults. Learn woodworking, a foreign language, simplified car repair, bookkeeping, local history, almost anything. Sometimes learning something new is the most fun of all—and useful to boot.

## TRAVEL AND RECREATION KNOW-HOW

People who travel a lot gradually accumulate lots of valuable tips and hints. Here are some of the money-saving ideas I've collected in my own travels or picked up from my travel agent.

## Eating out

- Study the restaurant menu before you go to a table. If the menu is not posted, pass the place by. Or ask to see one before being seated. Then you can be certain they have the kind of prices you want to pay.
- In almost every town there are casual restaurants that specialize in old-fashioned desserts. If you're budget watching but want to celebrate a special occasion, have dinner at home and go out just for dessert.
- Find out which restaurants in your area offer early-bird prices—special prices to the pre-5 P.M. crowd. Many restaurants have reduced prices for diners who order before a certain time. We found

an early-bird buffet at a hotel on the beach in Hawaii that was fabulous—a bargain for our family of six.

- Try foreign foods for fun. Some of the best restaurants in the world are inexpensive ethnic places. Try these out. Explore the interesting Oriental, Middle Eastern, and other low-cost exotic restaurants in your area.
- Don't double tip by mistake. Always take a moment to check your bill. If the tip is included in it, you'll be doubly glad you did. Many restaurants (in resort areas particularly) automatically include the tip when they are serving a group. My son, who has years of restaurant experience, tells me that many people double-tip even when they are told in advance that the tip is included.
- Fill in the credit-card total yourself. When you use a credit card to pay for a meal and the waiter/waitress brings you the form to sign and add the tip, do total the whole thing yourself. That way, there's no possibility of the restaurant charging more than they should. Also save your copy for comparison when your full statement arrives.

## Packing

- Post a packing list. Each family member should pack for himself, children from about age ten on. Make a packing list and post it for the family, so there's no excuse for forgetting something vital.
- Luggage shouldn't be a burden, so pack what you can carry! Buy a fold-up luggage cart to make carting your luggage around less tiresome. I wouldn't go anywhere without it!
- Leave valuable jewelry at home. On a trip it is merely one more thing to worry about.
- If you check your heavy baggage, make sure that valuables, cameras, documents, and important medications are packed in your hand luggage, which you carry aboard the plane or bus and stow under your seat. Checked luggage all too often travels in a different direction from you, and besides you may need to use these items en route.
- If you take certain outings regularly, make a permanent list of

things to take and tape it inside your closet door. We have permanent lists for skiing, camping, and sailing. I have a list for business trips I've used for years. It saves time in packing for a trip and saves you from buying forgotten items at high-cost hotel shops. You can imagine how much you will pay for sunglasses, film, or sun lotion in the Caribbean! So make up lists before you go.

---

### SKI LIST

| | |
|---|---|
| skis, boots, poles | ski sox |
| ski outfit | thermal undies |
| hat, goggles, gloves | sl. bag towel |

---

Buy heavy-duty nylon sports bags for your family members instead of more expensive luggage. Nylon sports bags hold a great deal, are lightweight yet strong, are washable, and can be carried by the handgrips or on your back. Moreover, they take less room in the car than boxy suitcases, and in emergencies they make better pillows. You can find them for about $10 at discount stores or sporting-goods stores. Buy a different bright color for each family member so bags can be quickly identified. You can write names on them with permanent felt marking pens. These nylon bags are great for sailing, skiing, and fishing trips too.

Be sure to have your name and address tags on each piece of luggage. If you are flying, the airline will provide free identification tags at the ticket counter, but otherwise make your own. It is a good idea to put your name and address inside the luggage also. If the bag gets lost and the outside tag is gone, airline personnel can identify it from an inside tag.

- Put racing stripes on your suitcase with vinyl tape so no one grabs it by mistake. So often a number of travelers carry identical suitcases and garment bags. I put a bright red-tape stripe on mine and saved myself lots of time and trouble.
- Take along: games, books, puzzles, decks of cards; addresses of friends and relatives; a small hot-pot or immersion heater and instant drinks; canned or bottled cocktails if you want a private drink without room service. We take Scrabble (pocket size costs about $4), backgammon, decks of playing cards and Mastermind. When our children were younger, we brought along card games like Crazy Eights and Old Maids. If you have young kids take along coloring books and crayons, crossword puzzles, and wordhunts. And if you never have time to do the crossword puzzles in the newspaper, start saving them in an envelope and then take them along on a trip. For the children, save the comics section from the Sunday newspaper. Take them along on trips and just throw them away when the kids finish reading them. Buy used children's paperbacks in a used book store and put them aside until you take a trip.
- Take your foam-plastic cooler along on vacation trips as well as picnics. That way, you can take lunch and cold drinks to the beach or parks, or as you drive, instead of buying lunch at a food stand or drive-in. If you're flying, buy one at your destination—they're quite inexpensive—and use this virtually weightless container to pack souvenirs or other extras for your return. The purchase price will be more than saved by not having to eat out.
- Use coolers as luggage. For our trip to Hawaii, we packed our snorkeling gear in our durable vinyl cooler, sealed it with heavy plastic tape, and checked it through as luggage. While we vacationed, we used the cooler for daily beach picnics, and at the end of our trip we loaded it with all the snorkeling gear again.
- Keep a first-aid kit. In a Baggie or tin cookie box, pack plastic bandages, pain spray, aspirin, and other medicines your family commonly uses, so you don't have to buy them at resort prices.
- Compare the cost of renting with buying equipment. It is usually

cheaper to rent equipment if you don't use it often or if you're outfitting growing kids. But we bought snorkeling equipment for the whole family for just a bit more than it would have cost to rent it just once.

- In summer, keep a basket packed with standard picnic equipment, ready to go along on a car trip at a moment's notice. All you have to add is food, then grab it and go. Your grab-it basket should contain some or all of the following:

    paper plates and cups
    paper napkins
    instant coffee, tea, sugar, dry cream
    plastic knives, forks, spoons
    1 sharp knife for slicing bread, cheese, etc.
    corkscrew
    bottle/can opener
    plug-in hot pot for heating water

You might want to include terry-cloth handtowels to use as lap napkins if you are eating while riding in the car. If you have small children—or even if you don't—carry a plastic sponge in a Baggie and dampen it just before you leave. It makes finger and face wiping easier all around.

## Sleeping accommodations

- Low-cost lodging is available if you are willing to look for it. Write to learn about these options:

**Youth Hostels.**
    AYH National Administration Offices
    1332 I Street NW
    Washington, DC 20005

**College Dormitories.** Many colleges now rent out dorm space during the summer. Call or write colleges directly to ask if they provide housing to travelers, Or write
    CMG Publishing, Inc.
    Box 630
    Princeton, NJ 08540

**Home Swap.** Trade your home for someone else's, and everyone gets to save.

> Vacation Exchange Club
> 350 Broadway
> New York, New York 10013
> > or
> INNter Lodging Co-op
> Box 7044
> Tacoma, WA 98407

**The Y.** Many YM or YWCA facilities have rooms for transients.

> YWCA
> 600 Lexington Avenue
> New York, NY 10022

- Compare the cost of a room with a kitchenette to that without. During a week of tennis or beaching you can save money by eating breakfasts in and packing your lunches. Then you might eat dinner out about every other evening. The increased cost of a room with a kitchenette will be more than compensated for by avoiding restaurants for every meal.

- Request the kind of hotel room you desire—on the sunny side, with a view of the sea/mountains, up high or down low. I'm afraid of fire, so my standard request is for the 2nd to 5th floor, near the elevator, with no extra doors between me and it.

- Hotels and motels in the same area can have prices that are very different. Shop around to get the best price. Once you decide where you want to stay, find out if they have rooms at different rates. If you do not ask, you may be placed in a deluxe room when economy rate rooms are available.

- Protect yourself from theft. Hang the "Do Not Disturb" sign on your door whenever you leave your hotel room. Anyone in search of a vacant room to ransack will not choose your room because they assume it is occupied.

- Don't advertise that you are alone. Some hotels have a paper doorknob tag for ordering an early-service breakfast. If you are a woman travelling alone, make certain that your doorknob tag does not advertise that fact. I always sign a man's name to the breakfast order—like "Rocky De Angelo." When breakfast is delivered in the morning, you can sign the charge slip with your correct name.

- Insist that hotels honor your reservation. Hotels will hold your reservation only until 6 P.M., unless you have guaranteed it with your credit card. If you have guaranteed it, they should hold it past 6 P.M. but will charge you if you do not show up. I always guarantee my room, and yet I have had hotels sell it from under me, guarantee or no. If that happens to you, demand a room, and keep demanding until you are convinced that every room in the place really is occupied. I usually tell the desk clerk that, if I'm not in a room within twenty minutes, I will put on my blue jammies and be sleeping on that couch in the middle of the lobby. That usually produces a room. But if there literally are no rooms available, the hotel must provide transportation to another hotel, where they know (by calling and checking) that there is a room for you. If the room in the second hotel costs more than your reserved room, the first hotel should pay the increased cost. Insist on it.

- Assert your rights as a paying guest. You deserve a room that is satisfactory, clean, and quiet. If there is a problem with your hotel room, insist on being moved to a different one. Toilets that would not stop running, doors that did not lock, the smell of wet paint, excessive noise—all these are reasons for requesting a different room. One evening, everything was quiet in my room until about 9 P.M., when the disco band started one level below. My employer telephoned me, and I have yet to convince him that I did not have a live band in the room with me. So, even though I had used the shower and unpacked, I requested a different room. It was move or stay up till 2 A.M. when the disco shut down.

- Always check your hotel bill before paying or signing the credit-card slip. Make sure the room rate is correct, the number of nights is correct, and that there are no long-distance telephone charges for calls you did not make.

# Traveling by car

Most people travel to and from their vacation site by car. Spend a bit of time, instead of money, to be well prepared for your trips by car.

- Buy a map and plan your route carefully
- Make Reservations at motels in advance so you don't get stuck with no room, or a high-priced room en route.
- Give your car a check up. Check oil, water, antifreeze, tires, spare tire . . .
- If your car needs repairs before the trip, have the repairs done at least two weeks prior to the trip. Then you can make sure it is running well before embarking on your vacation.
- If you are heading for snow country, make sure you have special equipment like an ice scraper, snow chains, bright flashlight for putting on chains at night, carpet scrap for kneeling in snow to put on chains, and extra antifreeze. Learn how to put on chains and do a practice run at home.
- Learn how to change a flat tire. Practice it at home.
- Take items you don't need out of the car trunk. Weighing the car down with unnecessary gear makes the car consume more gasoline.
- You can save money on car maintenance and operation by learning to add your own oil, antifreeze, pump your own gas, do tune ups, and check air pressure in tires. Consider enrolling in an auto maintenance class offered by adult education departments. Encourage your teenagers to take auto maintenance as an elective in high school. My daughter and three sons have all taken the class and found it to be invaluable.
- Keep an old blanket or bedspread in the back of the car. It makes a terrific beach blanket, picnic table cloth, or can be used as a handy groundcloth when you need one.
- Keep an extra umbrella in the car for surprise showers.
- Take along snacks and beverages in a cooler. This saves time, because you don't have to stop, and the snacks you bring along are less costly than buying something en route.
- Bring along games and books if you are traveling with young children. See ideas on page 104 for bring-along activities for children.

- On long car trips, when our children were younger, they were allowed to bring their bed pillow. Very handy for napping in the car.
- If you have an especially long drive with children, plan to leave very early in the morning. You load the car the night before, go to bed early, and then at 5 A.M. march the sleeping kiddies out to the car, and take off. You can get in a few hours of driving while the kiddies snooze before stopping for breakfast. This can make a long trip seem shorter to children.
- If you are traveling any distance by car, carry tissues, a roll of toilet paper, soap and towels. Sanitary facilities en route may be primitive or nonexistent. Carry pillows and blankets too. You may be stuck somewhere overnight—or passengers may just feel like a snooze as they travel.

# Traveling by air

Delays occur from time to time, no matter how you travel, but when you are flying you almost have to expect them. Make sure you understand what the airline is responsible for providing, so that, when you are delayed, you do not end up spending your own money. You should incur *no* out-of-pocket expenses because of cancelled or delayed flights, even when the reason for the delay is out of the airline's control (fog, snow, etc.).

- If your flight is delayed through a meal time, the airline will provide you with a voucher for your meal. But you will have to ask for it. Don't wait to hear an announcement about free meals. If you are delayed overnight, the airline is responsible for providing you with a hotel in addition to meals. But, again, it is up to you to ask for it. If you are told that there are no hotel rooms available, get on the phone and try to find one of your own and then get the airline to pay for it.
- In addition to providing food and lodging, the airline should provide you with a phone line on which to call long distance to tell your party on the other end that you are delayed. Simply say, "I need to use your phone for a long-distance call due to the delay."

- Never pay expenses and then go to the airline for reimbursement later. As soon as the delay is announced, tell them you need vouchers for meals and hotels. Then you don't have to waste time later writing letters for reimbursement.
- If you prefer, you may order a special meal at no extra cost. After you have made your reservation, call the airline and ask what special meals are available. Some airlines have only categories of meals available (low sodium, kosher, etc.) but not specific choices. Other airlines will actually read you a menu. I've had wonderful seafood plates or fresh fruit salads while my seatmate is munching the standard chicken and green beans. Call in your special meal request a few days in advance. Your travel agent can request the meal for you also.
- Reserve the seat you want: window or aisle, smoking or nonsmoking, forward or back. If you have underseat baggage, tell the reservation agent you must have underseat area (some parts of the plane don't have it). It is especially important to reserve seats if you are traveling with a companion, so you can sit together.
- Having a reserved seat does not entitle you to arrive late at the check-in gate. You should still check in about thirty minutes before flight time for domestic flights, an hour for overseas.
- Check your luggage in early enough that it makes your flight. However, if you are delayed and arrive at the airport just before flight time, do *not* check it in at the flight counter. Tote it with you out to the gate and tell the ticket agent there that it needs to be checked. You stand a better chance of getting it on your plane.
- If your luggage is lost, file a claim immediately. The airline must pay for essential items you have to buy (save receipts) to tide you over until you are reunited with your belongings.
- Have your tickets mailed to you. If you place your ticket charges on your credit card, you can order tickets by telephone with a travel agent or directly with the airline. Then the tickets can be mailed to you, saving you a trip to collect them. Some travel agencies will deliver tickets to your home or place of business. It never hurts to ask.
- Turn in unused tickets for a full refund. Once when the Philadelphia

airport was fogged in, I ended up chipping in for gasoline and driving there with other fellow stranded travelers. A week later when I returned home, I turned in the unused ticket to my travel agent, and my credit-card account was credited. You can also turn in tickets at the airline counter. This is true for all airline tickets except charter flights. Passengers who are holding tickets who simply do not show up may turn in those tickets for a refund. To combat this, the airlines oversell flights so they have maximum occupancy on flights. There is talk of charging a penalty fee to no-shows, but that policy was not established at the time of writing. A quick phone call to the airline on which you have the ticket will tell you if it is fully refundable.

## On-the-ground airport connections

- I travel to more than fifty cities each year without ever renting a car. Instead I pefer to use express airport buses, cabs, or limo service. Call your hotel or destination and ask which is the best way to get there from the airport without driving. When I go to an annual publishing convention in downtown Chicago, I catch an express bus at the airport, which drops me at the hotel door in forty-five minutes. I would not want a rental car even if they gave it to me for free.
- When you do rent a car, make certain that you understand how you will be charged. Is it a flat rate and unlimited mileage, or are you paying a daily rate plus mileage? Call or talk at the airport to several companies to find out which has the best deal. I recommend reserving a car through your travel agent. That way you can get the size of car you desire. A small car costs less to rent than a big one, and if you do not reserve ahead, they may only have the big monsters left. Without a reservation, you may get stuck without a car in a big city on a weekday.
- Ask the cost of the "drop fee"—the charge you pay for leaving the car in a different location from the place where you rented it.
- Get a free map from the car rental desk. They are usually found on

tear–off tablets on the counter. Car rental agencies at major airports have tear–off tablets with directions for driving from the airport to different parts of the city.

## Group power

- If you have a group who wish to travel together, talk to a travel agent about getting a group discount on transportation, hotels, car rentals, etc. Select the most articulate person in the group to negotiate the deal for you with the agent. Shop around with several agencies to see what is possible. Large travel agencies are probably in a better position to offer group deals and discounts than small ones.
- Share a vacation rental. Join with several families in renting a vacation house at a monthly rate and then divide up the days among families. (See p. 140.)
- Join a group or club that offers travel packages. We belong to a ski club but have never gone to a meeting. We pay a fee of $10 per person per year, which gives each member a booklet of discount coupons and a newsletter. The newsletter contains ads for ski weeks that are sponsored by the club at supersaver prices. We have skied at Vail and Aspen on package deals that include airfare, seven nights of lodging, and six days of lift tickets. Look at the group deals and compare them with what travel agents have to offer.
- Many airlines offer package vacations that include just about everything, so you know what the cost of the trip will be before going. Some vacation packages are scheduled tours where the whole group must stay together. But that is not the only kind of package available.

  Ask your travel agent to tell you about package deals for the kind of trip you hope to take. For instance, there are special package trips from San Francisco to Reno called "Gambler's Specials." They include round trip bus fare, coupons that may be turned in for a drink at the hotel casino, tickets for a show, and lodging for two nights. They have similar packages on the east coast to go to Atlantic City, New Jersey. A friend's mother took a fall foliage tour through New England last fall. It included round trip airfare from San Francisco to New York, two nights' lodging in New York, a Broadway show, and a bus tour through New England. The price for the whole package was a better deal than if she tried to set it up on her own. Find what is available by reading the travel section of the newspaper and checking with your travel agent.

- The package deal concept has been worked out very successfully for Club Méditerranée resorts. The price you pay includes transportation, lodging, food, sports activities, shows. Drinks at the bar are the only additional cost. When you go there, you know exactly how much you will spend, no matter how often you water-ski or sail their boats. All the recreational activities are included in the flat fee. We happen to like Club Med, but it certainly isn't for everyone. It has a silly reputation for being a wild place with groups of naked strangers running around. Not true! I've been to enough of their resorts to know. You can relax, enjoy sports and entertainment at no additional cost, enjoy sumptious meals and meet wonderful people from all over the world. Some of the Club Méditerranée resorts have special facilities for children.

## For senior citizens only

- Join AARP (American Association of Retired People) to get discounts on transportation, hotels, and some restaurants. Write for information to:

    AARP
    Box 2400
    Long Beach, CA 90801

- Telephone your local senior citizen center to find out what is happening for seniors in your area.
- Take day trips or trips around the globe with a few friends. It is more fun when you are not traveling alone, and being with others can also help defray costs, since you share cabs, rooms, etc.

- Write for information about Elderhostels held at colleges throughout the United States. You can take a week-long class without any
tests and live on campus reasonably. The information is free--why
not send for it?

> Elderhostel
> 100 Boylston Street
> Suite 200
> Boston, MA 02116

  Elderhostels provide an opportunity for senior citizens to live
together in a college dormitory, enjoy meals together and to take a
class or two. Class subjects vary from art history, Indian cultures,
writing, poetry, wood carving . . .

# Travel Agents

It does *not* cost more to use a travel agent. Agents get their income
from airlines, hotels, and car-rental companies, who pay them com-
missions. They can offer you many useful services and conveniences,
so you have nothing to lose by using them.

- Travel agents can alert you to special reduced fares that are
available. If you want the cheapest possible fare, say so, and the
agent will tell you your choices. If you have to bring some special
promotional fare to the attention of the travel agent, you are using
the wrong agent.
- Communicate to your travel agent how flexible you are on depar-
ture time, arrival time, dates, and willingness to change planes. The
more flexible you are, the more likely it is that you can take
advantage of special deals that save money.
- Plan ahead and save. The person who books a trip at the last minute
usually pays the highest price. Many special fares must be booked
for a certain number of days ahead. So give your travel agent
sufficient lead time to make the best deal for you.
- Approve your itinerary before tickets are made out. Ask your agent
to mail you a copy of your itinerary or read it to you over the phone,

so you can be sure it is the way you want it. Then tickets can be made out and mailed or delivered to you.

# While you're away

- Before you leave your house, set a timer so your lights go on and off, to make your home appear occupied. If you are not sure you will be back before dark, set the timer so lights come on in the evening. It is pleasant to come home to a lighted home or apartment.

  Having the lights go on and off while you are gone does cost money, but if it discourages burglars from selecting your house it is worth the cost. I think it is smart to make your home appear occupied when you are gone, as most police departments suggest. One little trick we do is to ask our neighbor's son to park his car in our driveway when we are away overnight. The fact that a car is sometimes parked in the driveway makes it look like someone is coming and going at the house.

- Pay a neighborhood teenager to gather mail, papers, and pet-watch while you're away on vacation, so you can concentrate on having a good time and avoid the possibility of expensive mishaps.

- Swap vacation housecare with a neighbor. You watch her property and feed her cat while she's away, and she will do the same for you. Works beautifully—we've done it for twenty years. If you have several animals, however, the hired-teenager is probably a fairer arrangement. Be sure to stock up on food, litter, heart-worm preventative, and all such other supplies before you leave.

- If you are able to camp at off-season, take advantage of the uncrowded parks. Friends, whose children are grown, do their camping at popular places like Yosemite in June and September when weather is good and the crowds are gone. Parks are crowded when children are on summer vacation from school.

- Ask yourself what are the activities your family will enjoy. If you love to fish, pick a spot to camp near a fishing area. Hikers should pick areas where they can take interesting hikes. You will want to do more than sit and watch leaves on the trees. Choose the area according to your interests.

## Where do you get all the gear?

- Consider renting or borrowing equipment for your first camping experience. Then buy used gear if you plan to continue camping.
- Ask friends if they have a list of stuff they take along that you can see. We have a separate list of clothing and another for food.
- You can rent a camping vehicle if you don't like the idea of tent camping. Some of the big camping vehicles are more deluxe than many homes. If you decide to rent a vehicle, check into renting it close to the area where you plan to camp. Then you won't have high gas consumption driving from your home to the area where you plan to vacation. We are tent campers and have never rented a vehicle. But we have friends who flew from California to the east coast, rented a huge camper and spent the entire summer touring in it. They loved it. At summer's end, they turned it in and flew home. They had a large family and saved money over staying in hotels and eating out.

## CAMPING VACATIONS PROVIDE LOW-COST FUN!

Camping is marvelous for family vacations. Campers can live away from home without paying hotel and restaurant expenses. Some of our favorite, best-remembered vacations were our camping trips.

## Where to go

- Talk to friends who camp. Find out their favorite spots and ask why they like certain areas.
- For your very first camping trip, pick a spot that is not too far from home and not too primitive or remote a campground.
- Find out the facilities that are available in the area you plan to visit. Are there showers, stores, hot water. . . .

Look at the campsite directories in the library. There are state, federal, and private campsite directories.

Make reservations in advance if you can. If the campground does not take reservations, time your arrival so you do not arrive at a peak time like the Friday evening before July 4th.

If you are staying in one camping area and plan to move to another without advance reservations, make your move mid-week instead of on the weekend when parks are crowded.

Jot a note to yourself about camping areas and particular campsite numbers that you especially like. Then you can return to the same spot another time.

Make sure you are prepared for all weather possibilities in the area you plan to visit. Find out about the weather before leaving home so you can bring rain gear, and proper clothing.

Check the newspapers for equipment rental. Some people who own tent trailers rent them out quite reasonably to defray costs.

If you are considering buying a costly piece of camping gear, such as a tent trailer, investigate the possibility of co-owning it with another person. See page 139 for ideas on shared ownership.

Teach your children how to roll up their sleeping bags at home. Then they'll be able to do it on the trip.

Practice using all your equipment at home so you are sure you know how it works and that it is in working order. It is difficult to try to light a camping lantern for the first time in total darkness. Practice setting up your tent in the back yard so you can do it easily on the trip.

Be patient with yourself. Every time you go camping you learn new tricks to make it easier and more fun.


## Clothing for camping

Bring dark colored, rugged clothing that you don't have to worry about. Blue jeans are perfect.

Bring rain gear along.

When our kids were tiny, I took raggy old shorts and pants along for them to wear on the camping trip. At the end of the trip, I threw the clothes away since that is what I was planning to do with them anyway.

- Bring a pair of old shoes for each child that can get wet. Part of the fun of camping for children is getting wet and dirty.
- Bring along plastic bags for damp clothing when you are packing up to head home.
- Bring a giant plastic garbage bag for dirty laundry.

# I'm hungry, let's eat

- Find out if ice is available in the campground. This will make a big difference in the kind of food you bring along.
- Freeze blocks of ice in milk cartons or buy block ice to keep your ice chest good and cold. Cubes melt faster. Keep ice chest out of the sun.
- Fill an insulated jug with juice so the kiddies aren't opening the ice chest frequently to get drinks.
- Use a permanent marker to write each family member's name on a plastic mug. Everyone uses and reuses their mug which cuts down on dishes.
- Enlist the help of the entire family on camp chores such as cooking and cleaning up after meals.
- Freeze batches of spaghetti sauce in a rinsed half gallon milk carton. It will help keep your ice chest cool and makes a great camping dinner. All you have to do is boil the pasta.
- Take frozen meats whenever possible so they keep well. Meats like hamburger should be used quickly.
- Plan your menu so you have meat meals immediately after going to the store. At the end of the week when you don't want to make another pilgrimage to the store, you can have boxed macaroni and cheese.
- Canned hams are terrific to take along on camping trips. Just put in the ice chest and it won't be damaged by the water in the bottom.
- Take along snacks to eat around the fire. You may buy things to use on camping trips that you don't use at home for the sake of convenience. I always buy those jiffy popcorn things that come in

foil pan. It's easy because you cook and eat the popcorn in the container. Perfect for camping. Buying snacks in campgrounds can be costly. Make purchases of things that are hard to bring along like fresh bread, milk and meats. You will pay more for these items in camping areas.

# 6

# SHARING THE WEALTH

By joining forces with friends, neighbors, and others, you can share many items you would otherwise have to buy, and everyone spends less. With just a little effort you can find people who want to team up to make their money go further.

# GETTING TOGETHER

Friends, neighbors and relatives all working together to save money. What a great idea! Once you start swapping, sharing, buying and bartering with other people, you will wonder why you didn't do it sooner! It's easy, it saves money, and it makes sense.

## wapping

Start a book or magazine swap box. Put a few paperback books and some magazines you have already read in a box. Leave the box in the coffee-break room at work, the laundry room of your apartment building, or any prominent spot where other people will encounter it. Mark it "Reading Swap Box" and put a sign on it that tells people they may borrow a book or magazine from the box *if* they put one in.

Start a swap box or rack for used sewing patterns or knitting and crochet instructions. Get your public library, club, or church group to sponsor it—it doesn't cost anything, and it may attract new members. Patterns or whatever can be borrowed on the honor system, and members can be solicited to contribute their old items. Our library conducts a twice-yearly used-book sale, books donated by patrons to the library's collection box. Thus people in the community have an opportunity to purchase used books cheap, and the library uses the money to buy more new books. Our library sale is organized by a group of volunteers called Friends of the Library, and if you want information about its national organization, write

> Friends of Libraries, U.S.A.
> c/o American Library Association
> 50 E. Huron Street
> Chicago, IL 60611

## Share a ride

Public transportation is the most economical way to get to and from work. However, it is not available in all areas, and in other areas some people simply refuse to use it. So, when you drive, offer to share the ride with others. More people transported for the same amount of gasoline.

• If you drive to work alone, consider getting a rider or two and share expenses. You could cover some or all of the costs of operating your car. Advertise for riders in the company newspaper and/or bulletin boards at work. Ask your personnel department to start a ride sharing bulletin board. Or post a notice with your phone number (only) at the local bus stop—with fare hikes coming in all the time, many people find that share-a-ride is not only more comfortable but cheaper than public transportation.

• Consider combining driving and public transportation. Many urban areas have park-and-ride lots on the outskirts of town, where commuters can park at low cost and then ride the bus or train into the downtown area. Talk your riders into trying it. Saves wear and tear on cars and drivers both.

• Become a rider in someone else's vehicle. Paying a driver will be less costly than operating your own car solo. If you want to have your own car one day a week—to do your banking, say, or go to the dentist—arrange to be driven only four days a week. Every day you do *not* drive alone saves you money.

## Volume discount

There is strength—buying strength—in numbers. If two or three families buy the same thing at the same time, they can do some useful cost cutting.

• When I was shopping around for a microwave oven, I learned that several of my friends were also getting ready to buy microwaves. Would they be interested in getting the same brand and model selected if I could get it at a lower price? The answer: *"Yes!"* I went to the store that had the best prices and negotiated the best price could get on the make and model I wanted. Then I told the saleswoman that I wanted a volume discount because I would be buying three of them. It took some haggling, but I managed to get an additional $50 off each oven.

- A fence contractor gave us a price on building a fence around our new house. My neighbor had a quote from another fence contractor on her property, which bordered ours. We decided to try to negotiate a lower price by having the same contractor do both jobs. First, without saying anything about our plan, we each got a quote from the other contractor. Then we proposed our deal to both of them and asked for the best price on doing both jobs. We ended up saving quite a bit of money, because it is cheaper in terms of time for the contractor to do two jobs in the same location. The fencing materials were all delivered at once, the posthole-digging vehicle had to be brought to only one location, and so on. I'm certain the same technique could be used for getting two solar-heating systems, landscaping jobs, patios, etc. It never hurts to try.

# Bartering

Virtually everyone has bartered on a one-to-one basis. If you have ever taken turns babysitting, or done a favor for someone in turn for her doing something for you, that's bartering. Bartering can give you access to goods and services you could not afford otherwise. You can barter with relatives, friends, neighbors, co-workers, church or club members. Formal bartering clubs can be established, although I have never participated in one—I prefer doing it one-to-one and setting the deal up myself. (By the way, the IRS does enter the picture. By law, the market value of what you trade is supposed to be reported as taxable income.) Consider these ideas for cashless swapping of skills and services.

- Share child care. This can be set up in many ways. You can form a babysitting cooperative, with monthly meetings and a set of rules everyone follows. Or you can work out an informal arrangement with friends, neighbors, or relatives. A major bonus for belonging to a babysitting co-op is that you have a group of people with whom you can swap information, trade or sell children's toys, furniture, clothing, patterns for sewing, outgrown bicycles, etc. There are books in the library about setting up a babysitting cooperative. Talk to friends who are involved in one to learn more about it.

For informal child care, ask yourself where your children would most like to be placed for babysitting. The answer is with their playmates. I worked out an arrangement with a neighbor. She watched my three- and four-year-old sons every Thursday morning from ten until noon while I grocery-shopped. I watched her boys for two hours on Friday afternoons while she had her hair done. No money changed hands, and we both got two hours of time free of children. During those hours, chances are our kids would have been playing together anyway. When our friends went to Las Vegas for the weekend, their four kids moved in with us (each one brought along a sleeping bag). When we wanted to go off for a weekend, our kids camped with them.

- Get what *you* want out of barter. A friend of mine has an elderly aunt who lives nearby. The aunt watches my friend's daughter every Friday night while the couple goes out for dinner. To pay her aunt back, my friend's husband cuts her lawn every week—which is what *she* needs done. No cash is involved, yet both parties get what they want.

- You care for the neighbors' pet while they are on vacation, and they care for your pet(s) while you are gone. Saves expensive boarding of animals at the vet, and the animal is probably happier on home territory. All you have to do is make sure the pet sitter has the name and phone number of your vet in case a problem develops. It is also a good idea to have the sitter feed the animal a few times before the family actually leaves.

- Give home permanents to your friends and receive gardening, cleanup, or shopping services in return. I've given at least two dozen home permanents—an art I learned from a friend—and consider myself to be quite the expert. Also, I taught my daughter, and she has given many a perm in the college dormitory in exchange for sewing and mending. One young man to whom she gave a perm tuned up her VW Bug for free.

*Tip:* If your hair needs to be trimmed, get it done about a week *after* the perm. Then if you have any fuzzy ends they will be trimmed. *Caution:* Never give a perm to anyone whose hair is tinted or bleached—that is best left to the experts.

- Exchange house sitting with neighbors. Water the plants and keep an eye on their house while they are vacationing, and they can do the same for you. If they have plants and you have a pet, you water their plants, and they feed your dog. Or vice-versa.

- Exchange home-improvement skills. Look over your (or your husband's) areas of expertise in carpentry, masonry, plumbing, electrification, sign and decorative painting, wallpapering and what-have-you, and see if any of your neighbors could use you in a swap deal—say, your husband's knack at car repair versus your neighbor's access to a backhoe—and get needed repairs or improvements done at the cost of the materials.

My husband became an "expert" at putting in underground sprinkler systems by taking a do-it-yourself class for $25 at a local building-supply and home-improvement store. (That $25 tuition was a credit that could be used toward purchasing sprinkler-system materials in that store, so actually the class was free.) Like most of our neighbors we could not afford to have our new house professionally landscaped. Instead, we were going to do it ourselves on the weekends. But once my husband had installed our sprinkler system, our neighbor was so impressed he offered to swap: a new sprinkler system for a new patio (he used to work on a cement crew during summers off from college). We leaped at the offer. We paid for all the materials for the patio, and he paid for all the supplies needed for his sprinkler system. About a year later, another neighbor showed us beautiful built-in bookcases he had crafted for his home. You guessed it: He built bookcases for our den in exchange for his sprinkler system.

Talk it up with friends, neighbors, relatives, and co-workers. What can you do? What do you want done that you can't do? Here's a list of possibilities:

## SWAP-A-SKILL LIST

cooking
bartending
serving at party/dinner/reception
cake decorating
flower arranging
singing, playing guitar or piano
pet care
pet grooming
child care
chauffeuring kids to appointments
bicycle repairs
car repairs and tune-ups
car washing and waxing
hair cuts
home permanents (men and women)
sewing/mending/alterations
furniture refinishing
painting
wallpapering
house watching
résumé writing
sketching/photography/collage making
typing
bookkeeping/tax preparation
deck building
patio construction
masonry
home decorating
sprinkler systems
carpentry/woodworking
plumbing
landscaping
gardening

# Group sales

Clean your closets, cupboards, and garage at a profit. Organize your friends and neighbors into holding a multifamily or group yard sale. Bigger *is* better when it comes to garage sales. Having a sale with other people is more fun *and* much more profitable. When you work together, you will attract more shoppers, share the work, and pay only a portion of the advertising fees. Best of all, you will make much more money than you possibly could by holding an individual sale. Talk up the idea with your friends and neighbors. People will see dollar signs when you offer them an opportunity to get rid of their no-longer-used possessions at a profit. Your unwanted items may be exactly what others are anxious to buy. Each person or family who participates is responsible for setting up and selling his own merchandise in his own front yard or driveway. Now for the secrets of success:

- Choose the best date: the first Saturday of the month at a time of year when you can count on fair weather. Many people are paid on the last Friday of the month, so they have money in their pockets then, and Saturday is obviously the best day for any sale. No need for a two-day sale. Make your money on Saturday from 8 A.M. until 3 P.M. Most serious buyers will be there in the morning.

- Organize the participants. After choosing your date, circulate a sign-up sheet among your group. Everyone who wants to participate must sign up, mark it on his calendar, and put $2 in the attached envelope. The money will be used for advertising. Get the advertising money up front. Then if someone decides to sleep in on sale day instead of participating, you still have his money. Should another party decide to join in at the last moment, collect ad money from him too. (In other words, there is no free lunch.)

- Give your advertising the Madison Avenue approach. Here's your chance to let your creative genius show. Make it glamorous and enticing. Certain words will pull people to the sale better than others. Here is my list of favorite words to use for yard-sale ads:

| WORDS TO USE | WORDS *NOT* TO USE |
|---|---|
| antique | old/used/secondhand |
| treasures | things/items |
| estate | house/home |
| colossal, huge, gigantic | big |
| bargains | cheap |
| rare, unusual, unique | ordinary |
| sports gear galore | baseball bat, roller skates |
| camping gear | lantern, pot |

In other words, make it sound like a happening that no one would want to miss. Which of the following ads will pull more people to the sale? (They have the same number of words, and therefore would cost the same to run in the paper.)

(a)

HUGE NEIGHBORHOOD
SALE—

antiques, unusual treasures,
unbelievable bargains in
this 12-family estate sale.
Be there! Merribrook Drive,
San Jose. Sat. April 1, 8–3 P.M.

(b)

NEIGHBORHOOD GARAGE
SALE—

Merribrook Drive yard sale,
several families, used items
for sale cheap. Merribrook Dr.
San Jose—please come! Sat.
April 1, 8–3 P.M.

Ad A is the winner, sure to pull people to your sale in droves.

Phone or mail ads in to the local and city newspapers. Indicate the date(s) you want the ad to appear. Do *not* include a phone number in the ad, or you will live to regret it. And don't forget to use community bulletin boards for free ads.

• Do not let yourself be talked into selling something for less than it's worth. That tearjerker tale of a dying grandson who could be made happy if only you'd let your prize guitar go cheap is probably just that—a story. Likewise, the man who says, "You want twenty dollars for *that* piece of junk?" is most likely just trying to get "that piece of junk" for next to nothing. If you know what some item is worth to most of your neighbors, stick to that price.

- Display advertising pays off, too. Delegate one participant to be the signmaker. The signmaker makes all the signs (and he'd better start saving cardboard immediately) and gets someone else to be the sign poster. Ideally, the sign poster is very tall, owns a staple gun, and doesn't mind getting up early. A few days before the sale, he goes around zapping up signs on telephone poles to direct people to the location of the sale. He also takes the signs down after it's over.
- Protect yourself from the dawn patrol. Some ordinary-looking people—could be your dentist, your children's teacher, or the local librarian—turn into garage-sale crazies once they hear of one going. They are so frantic to be first to touch the merchandise that they arrive sometimes hours before the sale begins and demand that you get up and sell them something. Don't let the frenzied dawn patrol get to you. Put a sign on your front door, before you go to bed *the previous night:*

ANYONE RINGING THIS BELL BEFORE 8 A.M. WILL BE
ELECTROCUTED.

or

GUARD DOGS ARE NOT LOCKED UP UNTIL 8 A.M.—BEWARE!

or

WE WILL NOT SELL ANYTHING TO ANYONE WHO COMES TO THE
DOOR.

In the morning when you go out to the kitchen to plug in the coffeepot, *do not turn on any lights.* The minute the lights go on, the crazies get out of their cars and swarm to your doorstep. (I speak from experience—I once made the mistake of getting the morning paper at 7:15 and was instantly rushed. They told me my clocks were wrong, and it was really 8:15.) Give yourself time to get properly up, dressed, and fed, and don't let *anyone* make you open up early.

- Carry all items to be sold into your yard or driveway and *close* the garage door. Then you won't have to worry about someone touching or trying to buy items that are *not* for sale. If you have the sale inside the garage, secure items that are not for sale.

- Some people say you must mark prices on everything. I never do. Instead, make a mental note of the bottom price you would take for some of the better items. When people ask the price of something, ask them to make you an offer. They will often offer you more than you would have asked.
- Should your sale be cash-and-carry or checks-accepted? Decide ahead of time if you will take checks. I do and have never had a problem. But with push-button banking and Saturday banking hours, most people can cash checks while you hold the merchandise for a short time, so accepting checks is not vital. But have plenty of change on hand so you don't have to dash into the house for it.
- Never hold anything for more than thirty minutes. You may never see those people again and be stuck with that purple lamp shade.
- Your house should stay locked while you are busy with the sale. You have no time to keep an eye on it. Don't let anyone use your phone or bathroom. Send them to the nearest service station.
- Show off merchandise to best advantage. If you have a radio or record player you are trying to sell, keep it playing. If Aunt Tizzie's pillbox hat is on sale, pop it on your head with the price tag dangling. That's what merchandising is all about—catching the eye. Or ear.
- Have fun at your garage sale. The best part of our annual group sale is the camaraderie of the whole experience. We get to talk to neighbors we rarely see. We laugh over incidents of the day and previous sales. Counting money at the end of the day is fun, too.
- Items you do not sell can be donated to the Salvation Army or Goodwill Industries and are tax-deductible.

# Food buying co-ops

In a food co-op, a group of people kick in to a central fund and then buy in quantity directly from the source. The savings can be impressive. Co-ops come in all sizes. I first thought about them when I overheard a friend telling someone she was "produce captain" for hers. She belonged to a co-op made up of hundreds of families with a produce division, cheese division, and so on—like a mini-General Motors with organizational charts, lists of rules, and lots of meetings. That was too complicated for me, but it gave me an idea for starting a more limited one.

The cheese co-op I established has twelve members and has been going strong for about five years. It takes no extra time and practically runs itself. But I did have to cut through some silly red tape to get the thing going. It is one of my favorite stories and so typical of dealing with city hall.

I telephoned the cheese company where we wanted to buy and was told that I needed to have a business license to buy there. That's easy, I thought, and called city hall. Business licenses were $35 (now, five years later, they cost $50), and no matter how I explained that our organization was not a business but a nonprofit food co-op, the code officer said, "Lady, you want a business license, you pay the thirty-five."

An annual fee of that size would make a large dent in the amount we saved, so I asked him to mail me the necessary forms, and I would think about it. When the forms arrived, I noticed that they said, "Fee: paid _____ waived _____." I filled out the form with my name and the name of our co-op, initialed it where it said "waived" with fictitious initials, crossed my fingers, and mailed it in without payment. I received the license within a week.

Every year I get a license renewal form on which I initial "waived," and I get the license. Who waived the fee? I guess I did. Here are the steps in setting up a food-buying co-op:

• Decide on the kind of food you want to buy. It is easier to handle things that are not terribly heavy, breakable, or frozen. Look in the yellow pages to see what is available in your area. I've heard of cooperative food buying for produce, canned goods, frozen vegetables and juices, meats, liquors and wines, cheeses and dry goods like rice, beans, flour . . . let your fingers do the walking to find out what is available in your area and don't let the red tape boggle your mind should you have to deal with city hall.

• Get your group of people together. Start talking the idea up to friends. Everyone in my cheese co-op lives in the neighborhood, which makes it very convenient to pick up the order. We have twelve members, which is enough to make up the $300 minimum order that is required by the cheese company.

• Try to buy from a company that will deliver. Ours delivers to the home of the person who placed the order. If you have a very large group of people ordering and you have to pick up the bulky merchandise, fitting it into a car may be a problem.

• Decide how often you want to buy. We buy about every six weeks. I make up a yearly calendar and photocopy it for everyone in our group. Every member knows the name of the person responsible for the order and must call his order in before the "order date." When the order comes in, members in our group must pick up the merchandise and pay for it between 3 and 6 p.m. that same day. Then the responsible person can zip to the bank and deposit the money to cover the check she wrote for the total order.

• Ask your dealer to give you a list of all the things they sell (a commodity list). Our cheese place also sells bulk spices, salami, pasta, and freezer paper in fifty-pound rolls at super prices.

• Some co-op buying is of necessity unpredictable. My friend, the produce captain, tells me they buy produce weekly. Everyone gives her $5 a week, and she goes to the produce market and buys the best bargains available that day. In other words, her members never know exactly what they will be getting, except that it will be $5 worth of produce bought at bargain prices.

• The important thing is to save money and to get food you would have bought anyway at a better price. Investigate the possibilities in your area, and don't let the red tape boggle your mind should you have to deal with city hall.

## Hire-a-kid (preferably one of your own)

Instill the idea early in the minds of your children that money is something you get for work. Instead of just giving kids an allowance, make them work for it from an early age. Kindergarten-age children can do tasks such as emptying wastebaskets, vacuuming, and dusting. They can be paid to babysit a younger brother or sister, so you are free to work or cook dinner without interruptions. Your own children are built-in helpers. I had a job chart for our kids, and jobs were rotated on a weekly basis. The children were *not paid* for these jobs.

In addition to their regular unpaid jobs I had a weekly job chart with the jobs listed and the price they brought. They were paid only if the job was done properly.

| | |
|---|---|
| sweep the garage floor | $1.00 |
| clean 7 sinks in the house | .75 |
| vacuum the family room | .75 |
| walk the dog | .35 |
| help put away the groceries | .50 |

- There are many benefits from hiring your own kids. They don't have to ask you for spending money, and instead of paying money to outsiders, you keep the wealth right in your own family. Best of all, your children learn the connection between money and work.

- Students make great helpers. If you want to hire a young person, telephone the high school or community college in your area to find out if they have a job service. Or take advantage of free advertising by posting a help-wanted ad (on a 3 x 5″ card) on community bulletin boards. If you are looking for a music teacher for your son who suddenly wants to play the drums, ask the high-school music teacher to recommend a student-instructor.

- When young people go out looking for a job (in an official interview or just to discuss the idea with a neighbor), they should go alone. Taking along a friend or two is *not* conducive to getting hired.

  Here is what else they should know: Be well groomed and neatly dressed. Get recommendations from teachers and other people for whom you have worked. Photocopy their letters of recommendation and take along copies to show people or to attach to employment applications. Out of several applicants for a bus boy job, my sixteen-year-old was the one hired, because he brought along recommendations from his paper-route manager, neighbors for whom he had worked, and a teacher. His employer joked about his "résumé," but he gave him the job.

- My children have been paid for a variety of jobs by friends, neighbors, and their parents. Here are a few:

### HOUSE JOBS

vacuum
dust
clean sinks
house-sit for vacationing family
paint room or house (or be painter's helper)
assist wallpaperer
wash windows
seal driveways (black asphalt)

### GARDEN JOBS

weed
water
cut grass
clean up yard
stack firewood
pick fruit or vegetable crop

### PET JOBS

pet-sit while owners vacation
walk dogs

### PARTY HELPERS

help at child's birthday party
play piano for adult party
serve
cleanup
bartend (over twenty-one only, please!)

## JOBS WITH KIDS

baby-sit

coach tennis, soccer, or baseball

walk young child to school

help someone who has new baby (mother's helper) (job might
be entertaining toddlers while dinner is prepared)

## OTHER IDEAS

sell coffee, tea, lemonade at garage sales

sell cold, canned soft drinks on hot days to people in gas lines
(during gasoline shortage)

grow and sell fruit and vegetables

cook, serve, and cleanup a main meal for your family

wash cars

repair bikes (my college-age son tells me kids who can fix bikes
at school have more jobs than they can handle)

run errands

stay with an elderly person (adult-sitting)

# OWNING/USING IN COMMON

You can tie up quite a few dollars buying all kinds of gear and
equipment. It is possible to spend less and still enjoy the activities you
like by buying used gear and by co-owning gear. Just take a look at
today's newspaper at the classified ads showing used recreational gear
for sale. You will be happily surprised to learn that you can buy all sorts
of treasures at super-saver prices. You might also think about advertising some of the never-used stuff you have cluttering up closets and
the garage.

# Save on gear and equipment

If you think you might like to try learning a musical instrument, camping out, SCUBA-diving, skiing, backpacking, or some such activity, rent or borrow the gear you'll need for your first experience. Only when you're sure you want to continue should you buy gear. Even then, look for good used equipment. "Used" need not imply "worn out." People have many reasons for selling their old gear: They want to upgrade the quality or sophistication; they've outgrown it or simply have no time for it anymore; the one who used it died or moved away; and so on. You can save at least 50 percent of the cost of equipment by buying it used or co-owning it.

- Make a phone call to sporting good stores that rent equipment and do some price shopping by telephone. Ask what kind of equipment they rent. I was amazed to learn that virtually all camping gear can be rented quite reasonably. What a great way to start out until you are sure camping is something you want to do often enough to invest in gear.

- Can you borrow equipment from someone to save money. Then if you want your own gear, you can watch the ads to pick up some good, used equipment. The best time to buy used equipment is in the off season. Small sailboat prices hit rock bottom in January and go high just before and during peak sailing season. Timing your purchases can save dollars.

- To buy used gear, check your local newspaper's classified ads for the kind of equipment you want. Or put up a notice on the bulletin board at work or your club. Also check "for sale" notices displayed by sporting-goods stores.

- Run a "wanted to buy" ad in the local newspaper. This is the way I locate used gear. I placed an ad in our local paper when I was outfitting the family for our first ski trip. The ad read:

> Ski gear and clothes wanted for
> kids: girl 12, boys 10, 8, 6.
> Call 555-4567

I got about five responses from local people, who had so many items their children had outgrown that they were delighted to get rid of them. At one house, after we selected quite a few things to buy, the couple insisted that we go through a trunkful of clothing and take whatever we wanted. I left with two bags filled with wool sweaters, hats, and at least six pairs of leather ski mittens. They refused to discuss payment for it—they were just pleased to know it was useful to another family.

- A sports equipment swap is a terrific fund-raising activity for organizations. Our neighborhood school had a swap for "sport stuff" that was run by the home-school club as a fundraiser. People were asked to bring their equipment to the school, where it was tagged and priced. The owners set the selling price and got a receipt for their merchandise. The sale was manned by members of the club and was held all day Saturday. The club paid the owners 80 percent of the selling price and kept 20 percent. Owners had to come to get their unsold gear and money for items sold between 3 and 5 P.M. after the sale. We got a check for the stuff they sold for us for over $75 after the club took its 20 percent. The sale included everything from bikes, tennis racquets, ski gear, exercise equipment, soccer cleats . . .

# Club up with co-enthusiasts

- Join a recreational club or group and enjoy your favorite form of relaxation at reduced cost. When recreation costs less, you can indulge in it more often. We saved a bundle by joining a ski club.

  When you add up the cost of lodging, gear, and lift tickets, skiing is a high-priced form of fun. We saved on gear by purchasing it used, and saved on lodging by joining the club and using its dormitory-style facilities. Instead of renting a condo for six people for $90 to $100 per night, we paid a $50 membership fee per family and then $5 per head per night every time we went skiing. For our family of six that's $30 a night instead of $90. The ski club has a big, fully equipped kitchen, so we can eat in. We do give up the privacy we would have in our very own cabin, but what we like about skiing is skiing down the mountain, not staying in luxurious quarters. So, we zip out of the club by 8:30 A.M. every day and return at 5 P.M. for dinner. After dinner, we just sit around the fire and talk to other families, and then crash about 9:30. Skiing as often as we manage to do it would have been prohibitively expensive if we had not joined the club.

- Think about renting a place in the mountains (summer or winter) or at the beach together with several other families. Then work out an arrangement for use (see also page 140). It could work in the same way our ski club did. Our club happened to be made up of about forty families, but you could do the same thing with just a few families or a group of singles who enjoy a common interest.

- If you own a house in a recreational area, get some extra mileage out of your property ownership. If you rent the property out, you may use it two weeks yearly for personal use, according to the IRS. Consider trading one of your weeks with someone who has a property in another area. We co-own a beach house with another family, so we get one week yearly for personal use. I am considering trading off four nights in our beach house for four nights in a ski house. I recently met someone who has a lovely ski lodge in my favorite area of Tahoe. No money will change hands—it will be a simple swap of time.

- Turn your private property into a club. You become one of the club's members, who happens to own the place. I talked to someone who has a fairly large place at Tahoe, which he converts to a club for three months of the year to reduce his costs. He gets two other families to pay him a fee that allows them to come up and use the place as a ski house any time they want to during January, February, and March. The owner and the two families who join the mini-club split the utility bills, snowplow service, and cost of firewood three ways. In addition, the two non-owners pay a rental fee. They have unlimited use and consider it to be a good deal. The owner likes it because he maintains control and yet reduces his expenses during the three months of the year when his bills are the highest. Smart!

# Share ownership

Through shared ownership you can be involved in recreational activities you may never have dreamed you could afford: sailing, motorboating, having a vacation cabin or recreational vehicle. The same concept works just as well for smaller investments like season tickets and seasonal equipment. Ticket sharing can enable you to see or take part in sports events, a ballet series, musical shows, drama series, a museum tour series, almost anything. And co-ownership puts you into possession of equipment you don't use often but find very useful when the time is right.

- Perhaps you would like to have season tickets for your city's professional basketball or baseball team. Tickets for the entire season, the cost of driving back and forth, paying a babysitter, and paying to park adds up to more than you can spend. So, consider buying a pair of season tickets with another couple—or two pairs of tickets co-owned among four couples.

Before the season begins, divide up the games evenly, giving each participant a certain number of week night and weekend games. If ten of the games promise to be especially desirable, take turns selecting tickets. Two couples can go together, sharing the driving to cut costs. Babysitting could be exchanged by the tickets' co-owners to cut or eliminate costs further. If ticket owners find they cannot attend one of their games, they could attempt to trade with a partner or offer a partner first opportunity to purchase them.

- If you don't use it often, buy it with a friend. One of the families we go camping with co-own most of their camping gear with a relative. The tent, stove, lantern, camping pots, pans, and utensils are all co-owned. Whenever they want to go camping, they use it, and if something gets broken or lost, they replace it. I co-own a large party-size coffee percolator with a neighbor. She keeps it in her house, and I borrow it whenever I need it. My brother and my parents co-own a Rototiller for the garden, since they live near one another, and it is something they both need only occasionally. Some canning equipment might be shared, too, although this is trickier, since both owners may need to do their work within the same limited time span. However, for people who put up only one or two kinds of food or are starting out small, co-ownership may help avoid a too-large initial outlay for kettles, nonmetal sieves, and so on.

- Buy a dream boat or a dream cabin. For many people, wholly owning a boat or a vacation home would tie up all their fun money. Because of this, they would probably feel guilty if they did not use the boat/cabin whenever possible. No matter how much you enjoy boating (or whatever), some of the fun goes away when you feel obligated to do it. One good answer is shared ownership.

Boats, a ski cabin, a private plane, recreational vehicles—all these and other such recreation items lend themselves beautifully to the co-ownership concept. Partners share equally in the cost of buying and keeping up the item. If it is purchased with a loan, partners each pay an equal portion of the down payment and an equal portion of the monthly charges. One person in the group agrees to be banker/bookkeeper, collecting the partners' shares and making the bank payments once a month. (The job as banker can be rotated yearly.) Costs for the upkeep, also portioned out equally among partners, must cover berth or hangar fees, insurance, taxes, and a repair fund.

An agreement must be reached about dividing up the use of the object. You may want to have a meeting every few months to assign days, weeks, or months when each partner gets his turn. Everyone jots down on his calendar who will be using the mutually owned object when. Then if one wishes to trade turns, he knows whom to contact. With a sailboat, you might use it only on Saturday, even though the whole weekend is rightfully yours. A partner, knowing this and wanting it for some special occasion himself, could call and trade off one of his days for your Sunday, and so on.

We got into our boat group through some neighbors. We owned a small sailboat that we used on a small local lake, but our dream was someday to own a boat we could sail on San Francisco Bay. Our new neighbors mentioned that they were part of a group of four couples who co-owned a big sailboat and invited us out sailing. We loved it. When one of the couples in the group left the area, we were invited to replace them. We agreed with some trepidation, being a bit spooked about getting out on the bay by ourselves. But our partners came along with us many times until we were skillful enough to cope with blustery San Francisco Bay.

At the time we were considering joining the boat group, we told some other friends about it. They laughed and said it would never work. Well, it does work. They are still wishing they could afford to buy a sailboat, and we are happily sailing our co-owned boat in the shadow of the Golden Gate Bridge.

- Take in a partner. If you already have too many dollars tied up in a boat or snowmobile you rarely use, sell half to a friend. Mention the opportunity for sharing ownership to friends, neighbors, co-workers, or advertise for partners. Your partners do not have to be best friends or people who live nearby. We know a couple who responded to a "co-owner wanted" ad in the newspaper, met the other couple, sailed on the boat, and decided to become co-owners. They never see the other people on a social basis; it is strictly a business arrangement.

- The same rules hold true for power boats as for sailboats. Co-ownership of a motorboat is especially useful for water skiers. If you know someone who owns a power boat and you wish you had one, suggest shared ownership. Most people are ready and eager to listen to an idea that reduces their costs by 50 percent.

- A major advantage of co-ownership is that it makes you plan to indulge in an activity on a specific day. When you schedule it on your calendar, you will tend to follow through and go. When you own your own boat, you might say to yourself that this weekend would be a good time to go out to the lake. Then something comes up, and the sailing gets put off till next weekend, and so on. But when it's your turn for a co-owned vessel, you go or lose your turn. The people who are the founders of our boat group tell us that they sail *more* as co-owners than they did when it belonged entirely to them. As boat co-owners, we found that we always went sailing on our scheduled days.

- Planning ahead is essential in co-ownership. A disadvantage of joint ownership is that you cannot spontaneously decide to go sailing (or whatever) without checking the calendar to see whose turn it is. If you are impulse-minded and dislike having to plan everything ahead, then co-ownership is not for you.

- Have a written agreement. It goes without saying, you need responsible partners to co-own something with. You will want to write out an agreement about maintenance and repair costs. For a boat, when the bottom needs to be painted or the motor needs a spring tune-up, it is paid for from the repair fund. If the repair fund cannot cover the expense, then everyone is assessed an extra fee. However, if one partner breaks something on board by accident or negligence, that person is responsible for repairing the damage.

- Co-ownership can give you an opportunity to learn new skills. As with us, your partners can improve your sailing skills. In addition to lowered costs, co-owning is a basis for friendship and camaraderie with people who share your interests. Some of our best, most fun-filled sailing days were the ones when we went sailing with our boat partners.

---

# 7

# SMART MONEY MANEUVERS

## Money maneuver no. 1:
## Be concerned with costs

Like businesses, individuals and families have to focus on costs, planning, and using credit wisely for sound money management. In today's inflationary world, it's more important than ever to get full

143

value for every dollar you spend and to know exactly what to do when you are a dissatisfied consumer. Here is the help you need for optimum money maneuvers.

- In any transaction for goods or services, ask for the price *immediately*. Before scheduling an appointment with an attorney, find out his/her rates. Before handing your shoes to the shoemaker for resoling, find out the cost of the repair job. Let the other party know you are dollar conscious. There is nothing "tacky" or "cheap" about asking for cost information. It is your money and you have every right to be concerned.

  The salesperson assumed we wanted a pin stripe down the side of our new car and implied that it came with the car, like wheels and an engine. We insisted that he find out the price difference without the stripe, and much to our amazement, the silly line of paint came at a cost of $200 extra. No thanks! We saved that much money by asking a simple question about cost.

  The clerk at the bank told me to look through the check-selection book and show her the one I liked most. I told her I liked the seascape checks but needed to know the cost. They were $7.50 per two hundred checks. I asked to see the cheapest checks the bank offered, and she showed me a basic blue check in the back of the book at a cost of $3.50. A $4 difference is not much all by itself, but I don't want to pay twice as much as necessary for something as basic as checks. I can think of better things to do with my money.

  There is nothing wrong with buying seascape checks or pin stripes for your car—just be sure to have a clear understanding of what you are paying for those extras.

- Compute the cost of some things you plan to buy in terms of hours of work. My sixteen-year-old son Don tells me a new surfboard will cost him fifty-two hours of work. He computed his take-home pay per hour as a busboy and knows exactly how many hours he must work to pay off a new surfboard. That is a rather astute system for figuring out the true cost of an item. With a take-home income of $6 per hour, a $420 purchase will take you seventy working hours to pay for. Mmmmm—that's something to think about.

# Money maneuver no. 2:
# Plan your finances on paper

- Know the fixed costs you incur monthly so you know where your dollars go. Share the facts and figures with your family members, so they have an understanding of family budgeting. When you tell your teenager that a 20-minute shower is too costly, he will know what you mean because he knows your monthly gas or oil bill. Another reason for doing some planning on paper is that you can set a goal to save toward. You can make a good decision as to an amount of money to put aside each pay period toward your goal.
- Experts recommend having a cash reserve equal to 3 months' income. Then, if no money is coming in, you can make it for awhile. Automatic payroll savings plans help many people to save.
- Keep a record of important dates, events, and financial transactions in your family. My mother spent a great deal of time going back through records to get important dates she needed:

  when my father retired
  when they sold a particular house
  when they bought a new house
  when they received a check from the government for flood
  insurance
  when my father had eye surgery

  She suggests buying a little six-year pocket-planner calendar. You can jot down important events and transactions in the book on any appropriate date. Then you don't have to dig through old records or try to remember fuzzy dates. At the end of the six years, buy a new pocket calendar book.

# Money maneuver no. 3:
# Earn all you can

- Have an up-to-date notion of what is fair pay for the kind of work you do. If you are working hard but feel you are paid unfairly low, you have two choices: You can stay and suffer, or go on to better things. Balance out the advantages and disadvantages of each choice, and then decide which is right for you.

- If you plan to move on, start shopping around without quitting your current job. If you do find employment elsewhere at a better wage, you may prefer to tell your current employer what you will be earning. He/she may be willing to meet your new job offer in terms of salary.
- Don't feel guilty about wanting to earn more money. That is the reason people work—right? If you are unhappy about being underpaid, don't get sidetracked by a nice office or a hanging Boston fern in your office window. Go after that larger paycheck.
- No matter what salary is offered to you, always ask for more money. Stay away from discussions of salary too early. If the prospective employer asks for your salary requirements on the application, write "Negotiable." If he/she asks for your salary requirements in an interview, put them on hold by stating that you are not ready to consider salary until you know more about the position.

  My way of handling this is to state that my policy is not to discuss salary during a first interview. If you are asked what you are currently earning, repeat that you do not discuss salary in a first interview. You can ask the interviewer what the salary figures are for the position for which you are interviewing. If the position pays $18,000 to $20,000, you can start out by asking for $22,000 and not go any lower than $20,000. Be tough and get what you are worth.
- Get paid to learn about a new field. If you are considering a costly training program to become a travel agent, medical assistant, or computer technician, get a low-level job in that field first. You may be offered free on-the-job training, eliminating the need for the training program. Best of all, you will have an opportunity to find out if it is a field you like before plunking down your dollars for career training.
- Start a Future Job ideas file. Save clippings from magazines and newspapers and names of people who are valuable contacts. Then when you are ready to do something, or just think about making a job change, you can peruse your idea file. I'm perfectly happy in my

job, but I must admit I don't have a five-year plan. I'd love to work in television. Anytime I see an article or information about working in television, I tear it out and pop it in my Future Job folder. It doesn't cost anything to collect ideas and names of important contacts.

# Money maneuver no. 4:
# Get what you paid for

You can return merchandise for a full refund when you are dissatisfied. Or have it replaced. Here are the secrets of what I call creative complaining.

- Save sales slips and guarantees to make it easier to return items. The store is justified in wanting some proof that you actually purchased the item from it. See page 176 for information about setting up a guarantee file.
- Decide how you want the situation resolved before entering the store. Do not sound apologetic or uncertain. Say, "I want a replacement clock—this one worked for only two weeks." Do not say, "Can you do anything about this?" Tell them—confidently and firmly—exactly what you want.
- Speak to the manager or person in charge. Most salesclerks are not permitted to accept returns. If the manager tells you to contact the manufacturer of the item, say, "No, I bought the clock here. Therefore I want a replacement clock from you. This one worked for two weeks." Use the broken-record tactic—keep repeating what you want, even if they laugh at you. Do not back down from your firm request and do not get angry.
- Write down the name of the person you are dealing with. If you are making a complaint by telephone, tell the person you are making a record of the call, and you need the spelling of his complete name so you can write it down. If you have to return to the store when the manager is in, or if you must return a phone call, you can state that you spoke with Mary Green last Wednesday about the problem. You will boggle their minds with your record keeping. This will also come in very handy should you need to make a report to a consumer protection agency or go to small claims court.

If you have a sincere reason for dissatisfaction, you can get what you want by following the tactics listed above. It does take persistance and determination. Consider the story of my new carpeting.

My two-year old, wall-to-wall carpeting looked fuzzy and matted in all high-traffic areas in our home. I went to the department store where I'd bought it and told the department manager I wanted the carpeting replaced at no cost to me. I jotted down his name while he chuckled over my request and said there was nothing he could do. I had to return to the store to meet with the store manager, and he also thought my request for new carpeting was pretty funny. But, he did agree to have the carpet buyer for the department store chain come out to take a look. I kept a record of all letters and meetings with date, time, and cast of characters. The carpet buyer agreed with me (as he crawled around our house on his hands and knees) that the carpeting looked dreadful, and he reported that to the store manager. I then scheduled another meeting with him. I told him I wanted (you guessed it) new carpeting at no cost to me. He said he could provide new carpeting at *reduced* costs, and I repeated my demand. He said he could offer me the carpeting, but I would have to pay installation fees, and again I repeated my demand. In that meeting I repeated my request for new carpeting at least a dozen times. Guess what I got? New carpeting for the entire house at no additional cost.

- Consider writing a letter to a consumer complaint column if you have one in your newspaper. They select certain problems and print the problem and the solution they worked out for the customer.

- Call the state and federal consumer complaint agencies if you cannot reach satisfaction on your own. They are listed in the black and white pages of your telephone directory under "United States" and the name of your state. Look up "Consumer Complaints" or "Consumer Protection."

- Go to the public library. Take a look at books on how to get action on your complaints. My favorite author on this subject is Ralph Charell, *How to Get the Upper Hand.*

- If all else fails, go to small claims court and file a complaint against the store or the manufacturer or whatever. Check the library for advice books on winning in small claims court. It costs about $3 to enter the plea, and most companies will rush to give you your money back—or whatever you want—rather than go to the expense of appearing in court. (*You* represent yourself in small claims, but companies have to hire attorneys.) The one drawback here is that there is a limit to the size of the claim you can enter, and if you have been bilked of a really large amount, you may have to hire an attorney yourself and take the offending merchant to a higher court.

# Money maneuver no. 5: Use credit cards wisely.

- If you receive credit cards in the mail you do not want, cut them up before discarding them. Otherwise, they can be retrieved from your trash or found at the city dump and used for a few weeks. Avoid credit-card ripoffs.
- Cut up credit cards in at least four pieces when you throw away an expired card. That way it can't fall into the wrong hands and be used.
- Keep your credit-card number secret. Most mail-order companies will take credit-card purchases, and someone could easily use your name and number to order merchandise and have it sent to his address. After you have checked your copy of the credit card slip against your bill, tear up the slips (or burn them in the fireplace) so no one can retrieve your name and credit card number from the discarded slips.
- When using your credit card, make certain only one imprint is taken. Watch what the person does with your card. If he makes a second imprint, insist that it be destroyed in front of you. A dishonest sales clerk or restaurant employee could imprint your card twice, and then use the second slip for an additional purchase for which you would be billed.
- When you have your card with you, don't let it out of your sight. This is almost impossible in restaurants because they usually take your card away from the table. But there are two things you can do

for protection: check your bill to make sure double charges were not made and compare it with the total on the credit slip. Be sure they match and do not add up to a higher amount.

- Make certain that you get your **own** credit card back from salesclerks and waiters. It is possible for mixups to occur in busy stores and dimly lighted restaurants.
- Carry your card in a safe place. Some people like to keep credit cards in a separate card holder instead of in their wallets.
- Don't carry all your credit cards all the time. Carry a card or two that you plan to use. Keep other cards in a safe spot at home. When you are going shopping, you can take along your department-store cards.
- Keep your customer copy of the charge slip to check against the bill. Many errors and abuses occur—take a few minutes to check your bill carefully. Be on the lookout for extra charges that are not yours.
- Some people find it helpful to carry a small pocket calendar book in which they jot down credit-card purchases. This serves as a double-check record in addition to the sales slips. Just jot down the store name or restaurant and the total amount of the bill put on your card by the appropriate date.
- Lost or stolen credit cards should be reported immediately. Keep a list of your credit card numbers, and as soon as you are certain that your cards have been stolen or lost, report them. You are not responsible for *any* unauthorized charges made *after* you notify the card company. If someone used your card *before* you report it missing, the most you will have to pay, even if there are hundreds of dollars in unauthorized purchases, is $50 per card.
- Keep your cards at home in a *safe* spot. A friend of mine once noticed some charges on her department-store credit card that no one in the family could explain. To further confuse the issue, her credit card was right in the desk drawer where she always kept it. After checking with the store, she found out the purchases had been made in the men's department. She finally figured out that her card had been taken from the desk, used, and put back by a workman who was installing a new kitchen floor in her house. A

desk drawer right by the telephone is *not* a safe spot for credit cards.

- Make it a policy never to use your credit cards for purchases under a certain amount—$25 or $50. It is very easy to get into a buying frenzy with credit cards and buy lots of small items. They can add up quickly into hundreds of dollars.
- Make credit work for you. If you buy an appliance on sale using your credit card and set up a schedule of payments, you can save money. If you pay $30 in finance charges but saved $75 by making the purchase when you did, you came out ahead.
- Finance charges on credit cards are tax deductible. Don't overlook that on your income-tax returns.
- Always compute the cost of credit financing before making a purchase if you plan to pay over time.
- The federal government has free pamphlets on using credit cards, on truth-in-lending laws, on filing consumer complaints, and so on. Write for a list of available titles:

  Publications Services
  Division of Support Services
  Board of Governors of the Federal Reserve System
  Washington, DC 20551
- The Bank of America also has free consumer-information reports at many of its branches. Or you may write:

  Bank of America
  Specialized Services
  Box 37128
  San Francisco, CA 94137

## Money maneuver no. 6: Keep track of tax deductible expenses.

- Buy a pocket calendar booklet for the year in a stationery store. They cost about $2. Staple into the booklet receipts and jot down car mileage that is tax deductible. I used to make a half-hearted attempt to keep track of business expenses I incurred as a writer, but I would lose receipts or find them in the bottom of my purse and not recall what they were for. My husband Walt suggested that I use the pocket calendar booklet and it works like a charm. I staple in by the date I incurred the expense, receipts for postage, paper supplies, typewriter ribbons and service, and so on. I jot the mileage down too. I keep the booklet in my purse so it is always handy.

# 8

## TAKING GOOD CARE OF YOURSELF

Good health is up to you. Make a commitment to healthier living by eating a nutritious, well-balanced diet, by following a sound exercise program and by keeping well informed on health matters generally. If you maintain fitness, you'll find that you generally have to spend less on health care. Also, a healthy diet (more vegetables and grains and less meat and fats, less alcoholic beverages, fewer over-the-counter drugs, etc.) tends to be easier on the pocketbook than unhealthy eating habits.

# AN OUNCE OF PREVENTION

The best way to stay well is to practice preventive medicine techniques. That means staying informed about what makes for healthier living and making changes when they seem necessary. You'll be richly rewarded by feeling better and enjoying life more.

There is nothing you can do to *guarantee* that you will always be healthy, but you make it a lot more likely by doing everything you can to maintain your family's health. Currently doctors are advising the following guidelines:

Eat less salt (linked to high blood pressure)

East less fat (linked to heart disease)

Avoid excessive sun exposure (linked to skin cancer and premature aging of the skin)

## Eat healthful foods

- Start reading and listening to articles in the media on good nutrition.
- Borrow books on healthful eating from your public library.
- Build up a collection of interesting recipes for healthful meals (consult newspapers, magazines, government bulletins).
- Call the American Heart Association for information on proper diet. It is listed in your telephone directory.

## Maintain your optimum weight without medication

- Eat more vegetables and whole grain products. Reduce intake of fats and sugar.
- Don't waste money on fad diet books or medications.
- Call your physician to find out a weight-loss diet he/she recommends.
- Find out about joining a support group like Weight Watchers. They are listed in your telephone directory.
- Diet with a friend and chart your progress.

# Keep yourself fit

- Walking (the pace should be brisk) is terrific exercise, and it's absolutely free. While you walk, see the sights, bird watch, window shop, get to know your neighborhood. Walking can also save money. Walk all or part way to work or to the market. Some senior citizens who are unable to get outdoors in bad winter weather to walk do their walking in shopping center malls.
- Clip articles from newspapers or get books from the library on exercise.
- Buy or borrow an exercise record or tape.
- Get an exercise partner and set up a scheduled time to work out.
- Take an exercise class. Find out if your community college or local hospital offers classes at low cost.
- Swimming, bicycling, jogging, skating and jumping rope are excellent components of an exercise program. Take a ballet or tap dancing class on your own, or a ballroom dance class with a friend. Check with the city recreation department and community colleges to find out about lifetime sports and exercise programs they offer.

## Getting naturally good sleep

- Sleep is natural and should not require sedation. With good diet and exercise, you should be able to get a good night of unmedicated sleep.
- Stop napping or dozing on and off all day. If you need a nap, set aside a brief, regularly-scheduled time each day.
- Establish a regular schedule for going to bed and rising.
- Exercise to reduce tension and aid sleep (not right before bedtime because exercise usually wakes you up.)

## Stop smoking

- Call the American Cancer Society and/or American Heart Association to find out about stop-smoking programs they offer. Ask for free literature that is available. Giving up cigarettes is one of the best possible ways to save money.

- Find a partner to quit with you. Then you can keep tabs on one another's progress.
- Get library books that tell how to stop smoking.
- Call your local hospital to find out if they offer programs at low or no cost to help smokers kick the habit.

## Go easy on alcoholic beverages

- Switch to light wine punches, wine and soda, mineral waters, or vegetable juices—all are lower in cost than liquor and better for you.
- Always have nonalcoholic alternatives available for your guests when you're entertaining. Try herb tea mixed with fruit juice for interesting combinations that are easy on your budget.

## Don't take unnecessary drugs or medications

- Seek actual solutions to problems instead of medication. A staggering amount of unnecessary medication is sold, at astronomical prices, to alleviate everything from jittery nerves to constipation.
- Think of drugs and medication as something you prefer *not* to have in your body. And something you prefer *not* to have to pay for.

## Buckle up your seat belt

Get in the habit of using your car seat belt—no matter how short the trip. As a passenger in someone else's vehicle, make a point of finding and getting into the passenger seat belt. Other passengers will wear a seat belt when you do.

## MEDICAL CARE

Informed patients get the most for their money from medical and dental services. Learn how to establish a partner relationship with your doctor and dentist. You should understand the whys and wherefores of the care you are getting. After all, it is your body and you are paying the bill.

## You and your doctor

- To select a physician, check with friends. Find out why each one likes the particular doctor she goes to. Then telephone, or stop by the office, to find out if he is relaxed and easy to talk to. Your physician should be approachable—not someone who makes you nervous and ill at ease. Don't hesitate to ask questions. Ask about fees. For instance, if you are seeking a new gynecologist, ask for the cost of a standard check-up and PAP test. Then you can compare the cost with another practitioner. After all, you are paying the fee, and it is your body.
- Match your doctor to your philosophy of health care. Some physicians do more diagnostic tests, prescribe more medications, and require more office visits than others. Even if these things are covered by insurance, you may not want to subject your body to more medication and testing than necessary. I prefer a physician who practices conservative medicine. Conservative physicians will not prescribe over the telephone or give you medicine because you ask for it. They won't send you to the hospital at the drop of a symptom. Other people may dislike my doctor for the same reason I happen to like her. You must find a physician who satisfies your personal needs.
- If you need a specialist, you might want to request a clinic or medical school in your area to make recommendations. Get at least three names. Or ask your own doctor for the names of two or three specialists in the field you're interested in. Generally speaking, universities and teaching hospitals will be aware of the best physicians in a given specialty.
- Change doctors if you are unhappy with the care you receive. Shop around for another doctor by talking to friends. Then sign a release with your new physician to have the records transferred from the other doctor. There should be no fee for transferring medical records. X rays may also be transferred—you paid for them, and they belong to you.

- Ask in advance about your doctor's fees. Make sure you understand what is included and what is *not* included. Ask for an explanation of any item you do not understand on your bill.
- Phone your doctor for advice instead of going in for an office visit whenever possible. You may have to state the problem to the nurse and then get a return call from the doctor, but the phone call can occasionally replace an office visit.
- Be prepared for medical emergencies. Find out how to get medical help when the doctor is not in his office. Virtually all of the accidents and medical crises in our family have happened on weekends and evenings. Knowing what to do and how to contact your personal physician can save an expensive emergency-room treatment.
- Before you have diagnostic tests done, do some fact-finding. It is your decision whether to agree to the testing, so be informed about them. Ask you doctor what information will be gained from the tests he wants to run, what risks the test procedure carries, how much it will cost. If the test is expensive or risky, you may want to get a second opinion before giving consent.
- If you are already in the hospital, or entering the hospital, ask your doctor which tests are absolutely necessary. Have the physician give you a list of the testing procedures that should be performed. Ask questions about tests before they are performed. If you are about to be tested for something that is not on your list, start squalking and say STOP until you doublecheck with your physician. There should be a reason for tests. "Routine procedure" is not what I call a good reason.
- Let your physician know from the beginning of your relationship that you plan to be an informed patient. After all, it is your body and your money. If you do not understand what your physician is saying, ask him to explain it in a different way. Say, "I do not understand what you mean. Please explain it in a different way. Perhaps drawing a sketch would help." Never hold back on questions because your doctor seems too busy.
- When surgery is recommended, get a second opinion. (The exception to this is emergency surgery when time is of the essence.) Many insurance companies will pay for a second opinion before surgery. Go to a doctor that is not affiliated with the same medical

group or hospital as the first doctor. Don't tell the second surgeon that his is to be a second opinion until after you get it. Then you can explain to him that it supports or disagrees with the first doctor's recommendation. Physicians do not like to contradict one another. Therefore, it is best not to place them in that position by asking them to validate what another physician recommended.

- Yearly physical examinations are unnecessary for most healthy individuals. Many physicians nowadays consider yearly physical exams to be a waste of time and money. Ask your doctor which procedures or tests he considers to be important enough to be checked anually. Depending on your age and life circumstances, they might include blood pressure, glaucoma, pap smear, and so on.

- Your medical records belong to you. You can have the records and your X rays transferred to another doctor if you wish to change. This can eliminate the need for a second set of X rays, saving you from spending money and getting more radiation than may be good for you. The American Medical Association advises against unnecessary X rays.

# Outside help

- Research shows that a network of family and friends who lend emotional support in times of crisis can help you more, or as much, as professional counseling. It is perfectly okay to ask for emotional support from people when you need it. Friendship is not only for the good times. Pretending you are "just fine" when you aren't is an unhealthy, destructive way of handling trauma.

- Get a handle on your worries. Block off "worry time" if you must. If you are a wreck because your salary review is on Wednesday afternoon, block off Wednesday morning, from the minute you wake up, as worry time. That will get you off the hook until Wednesday afternoon. Read up on the art of worry reduction. The public library has many self-help books on stress reduction.

- Some people are unpleasant, negative complainers who leave you feeling stressed after being with them. You know the people I mean, you can count on them to be in a bad mood virtually all the time. It is important to learn how to handle people whose behavior is exploitive. Learn how to cope with difficult people. Read library books on assertive behavior or take a course in assertiveness training. Practice a few simple lines for handling people who complain or criticize. For example: "Thank you for sharing your feelings with me. I hope you can solve your problem." You have acknowledged their feelings but have not allowed them to hand you their problems.

- Surround yourself with positive people. Negativity is contagious. Some people concentrate on being well, and others thrive on illness. Pick the ones who enjoy good health and sidestep those for whom happiness is having something to gripe about.
- Train your children not to make a fuss over pain. If you react to every little scratch, children learn to use injury or illness to get attention. When I was teaching first grade, I had some pint-sized hypochondriacs who went through my year's allotment of Band-Aids in the first month of school. Hence I developed the rule, "No blood, no Band-Aid." Emphasize other, positive ways to get attention.

## Medical and dental insurance

- Make the most of your policy. Does it cover your kids who are away at college? Are prescription drugs included? Find out so you get full use from your policy. If you have questions after reading the policy, write or call the insurance company to get answers.
- Don't pay for the same coverage twice. For example, my husband's group medical and dental plan offered through his employer pays for all his dependents up to age nineteen (or twenty-three if they are full-time students). The fee for the coverage is paid by the company and not deducted from his paycheck. My employer pays for me, but coverage for any dependents is an extra fee that I would have to pay. We elected *not* to pay extra to have our dependents covered on my plan because they are adequately covered under my husband's company-paid plan. If both our plans required us to pay extra for dependent coverage, we would compare both plans and choose the one that gave the most coverage at the best rate. Don't duplicate coverage.
- Don't get caught between jobs without insurance. If you leave your

job, make certain you continue your insurance until you are covered under a policy by your next employer. If you have a period during which you will not be covered, it is worthwhile to buy a conversion policy on the coverage you had with your previous employer. The important thing is to avoid having a period during which you are *not* covered by medical insurance.

# Medication and prescriptions

- Many physicians say that patients expect to receive a prescription for medication as part of a visit. Getting medication seems to help the patient justify the fact that he went to the doctor in the first place. Don't ask for medication. If you need it, your doctor will tell you. Consider yourself fortunate if you do not need a prescription for medication.
- Ask your doctor to write the prescription for the generic drug instead of the name brand. What is the difference between brand names and generics?

  Brand name: Valium
  Generic name: Diazepam

  You will pay considerably more for the name brand.
- Ask your doctor questions about your prescription:

  What kind of medicine is it?
  What results should you expect?
  How often should it be taken?
  Should it be taken with food or on an empty stomach?
  Are there side effects to watch for?
  Are there any incompatible foods or medications?
- Tell your physician you want the smallest amount of medication that is possible. When my son had a wisdom tooth removed, the oral surgeon gave him a prescription for codeine. Instead of getting it filled en route home, he waited to see if he needed it or not. He got sufficient relief from aspirin and discarded the prescription. If it had been a deeper-rooted tooth, of course, he might have needed the stronger painkiller, but since he didn't need it, he didn't take it. A sensible policy.

- When you visit your doctor, take along any medication you are using so he/she can take its effects into account when he examines you.
- Shop at discount pharmacies instead of small, local drugstores. When my daughter bought malaria-preventative medication for a student trip to Africa, her pills cost about $20. Other students in the group paid between $20 and $48 for the exact same pills. What made the difference was the place where they purchased the medication.
- Shop to get the best price. If you know the name of the medication, quantity, and strength, you can price-shop by phone. Or take your prescription to several pharmacies and get the prices. Then buy it where you get the best value.
- Ask the pharmacist the same questions about the medication that you asked the physician. The pharmacist may have more information that is helpful to know.
- If you use large quantities of a certain medication, find out if you can buy a big batch all at once. Sometimes buying in larger quantities can mean getting it at a lower cost.

## Hospitalization

- Tell your doctor you want to do everything you can to keep costs down. Ask your doctor what is the least amount of time you can spend in the hospital if everything goes well. Find out about check-in and check-out times, if you stay past a certain time on check-out day, you are charged for another day as if you were staying at the Hyatt Regency.
- Find out the price-per-day for different types of rooms (private, semi-private, ward). Decide how much you want to pay, on the basis of what portion of the cost is paid by the insurer. Read your policy to find out ahead of time and then order the kind of room you want.
- Ask if the hospital procedure can be done in the outpatient clinic to cut costs.
- Hospital pharmacies tend to be high-priced. Get your prescription filled elsewhere. The same thing is true for pharmaceuticals. If you

are an inpatient and need a heating pad or sanitary napkins, get a friend or family member to go to an outside store instead of buying it at the hospital pharmacy. The $15 heating pad from a discount store might cost $30 in the hospital pharmacy.

- Take items home with you from the hospital if they are going to be discarded anyway. Ask the nurse about the plastic items you used, such as tray, pitcher, bowl, etc. If these are throwaway, take them with you. You paid for them, didn't you?
- Check your bill carefully. Do not hesitate to question any item that seems dubious.
- You have the right to question your medical insurance payment. Make certain you get the coverage you are paying for.

# You and your dentist

- You are a consumer when you buy dental and medical care. Ask questions about treatment and costs before procedures are done.
- Ask for recommendations of dentists and orthodontists from friends, from your physician, or from your county dental society.
- Request free instruction on proper brushing and flossing from the dentist or hygienist.
- Ask why treatments are necessary, how much they will cost, and if there are alternatives to a certain procedure.
- If your dentist suggests a major, expensive program of treatment, get a second opinion. Go to someone who is not in the same group or building. If X rays will help the dentist evaluate you, have them sent by your other dentist. If the second dentist recommends the procedure that was suggested by the first dentist, get a price quote.
- Take a toothbrush and toothpaste to work so you can brush after lunch.
- If you are concerned about paying for dental care, work out a payment plan with the dentist before the procedure starts.
- If money is tight, ask your dentist if the work can be postponed safely until you are better prepared to pay for it.
- If you have dental insurance, make sure to have checkups at the suggested intervals, so coverage remains at the maximum level.

Some policies will pay a higher percentage if checkups occur at least once a year. Mark the calendar and stay on schedule to get the most from your insurance.

- If you change dentists, have records and X rays transferred. There is no reason to pay for a second set of X rays when you already own a set.
- Tell your dentist that you want as few X rays as possible. If he insists that X rays are necessary at each visit, you may want to find another dentist.
- Orthodontia can result in a healthier mouth. It is not purely cosmetic. My braces were put on at age forty-one, and I wore them for two years. I only wish I had done it sooner.
- Get price quotes from at least two orthodontists. Find out if there is a one-time charge for the treatment or do you pay a monthly fee for as long as you are under treatment. I shopped until I found an orthodontist who would give me a fixed price for treatment. Even though he said he normally does not do that, he was willing to negotiate that with me. It never hurts to ask. Maybe all those kids with crooked teeth in our family influenced his decision.

# 9

# SLASHING SERVICE COSTS

Everyone is talking about rapidly rising monthly bills for gas, electricity, telephone service, and repair bills. You can do something about it. You can slash service costs without cutting conveniences. With just a bit more awareness and an assertive attitude you will soon be an energy saver. The tips here show how to reduce some costs, and avoid others entirely. You can implement many of them immediately.

# Phones and Phone Service

Telephones now come in so many sizes, shapes, colors, and styles that they would boggle the mind of Alexander Graham Bell. The telephone has become a status symbol and objet d'art. Both the telephones themselves and a variety of phone services are merchandised masterfully in the telephone-company stores. Those smiling service representatives are actually salespeople working hard to sell you the most phones and the most service. So when you're considering phone service, arm yourself with information to make sure you get the most for your money. Take as much time as you need and consider carefully the options available in equipment and service.

## The right equipment

- Make sure you understand what you're paying for. The rental fee for a telephone is a separate charge from the service fee. Ask a phone representative to break down the costs so you know exactly how much each item comes to every month. Jot down information and prices as you talk, then you can make careful price comparisons.

- Ask the phone company representative for information on the cheapest phone and the cheapest service. The least expensive telephone available will probably not be displayed center stage in the company store. If you don't see the basic boxy phone with a dial, ask for it, and they will fetch one for you. It comes in colors at no extra charge, but there is a smaller choice of colors. If all you want is a telephone, this may be your most sensible choice.

- Own your own phone. You do not have to continue renting a telephone from the phone company. You can buy your own—either one from the phone company itself or one manufactured by an outside source and sold at discount stores, electronic equipment outlets, and even supermarkets. The telephone company will repair its own equipment, both the lines and the instrument, but it will charge you for repairs to the instrument if you are the owner. (If you continue to rent, repairs to the instrument will be free, too, as always.) Most breaks in service, however, are in the lines.

Buying your own telephone can be a saving in the long run. Phones cost anywhere from $20 on up, but those rental charges ($2 a month and up) mount steadily, and by saving them you can probably pay for that purchased phone in less than a year. Or two years if you opt for a high-style instrument. From then on, the cost is free and clear.

If you decide to buy the telephone company's instrument, make arrangements at the phone store. If you prefer to buy at an outside source, call the business office of the phone company and ask them what the local procedure is. They will need to record the registration number on the new instrument and arrange for its installation. From then on, you will pay only for your use of the company's lines.

- Phone accessories like jacks, long cords, and automatic dialers are also available in discount stores. They are priced much cheaper than at the telephone company store.

- My neighbor has a phone with "call waiting" service. "Call waiting" signals you with a clicking sound when another call is coming in, so you can put the party you are speaking to on hold and answer another call. But for less money than she's paying now per month, my neighbor could buy her own phones and have two separate phone lines instead. Shop and compare, and you will get maximum service for your money.

- "Call forwarding" is another service that comes at a monthly fee. I'm sure it is invaluable for some people who must be available in case of an emergency (like an obstetrician on call). But if your calls are not urgent, consider buying a telephone-answering machine instead, which is like a secretary taking your calls. Remote control devices are available so that you can even call in and get your messages from a different location. The telephone company store sells answering machines, but they can be found elsewhere at much better prices.

- When my daughter Sue ordered telephone service for her college dorm room at the telephone company store, she was told that everyone gets the "standard dorm package," which (surprise!) turned out to be an expensive phone and high-priced service. Despite that she requested the cheapest phone and the cheapest service and she got them. Everyone else in the dorm got the "standard dorm package" and laughed at her for her "funny phone." Well, her "funny phone" happens to cost *half* as much as the so-called "standard dorm package." So don't be intimidated into accepting some mythical standard package if rock-bottom prices are what you want.

- Request an extra phone directory for another room of the house. They are available for the asking from the telephone company. They will also provide a free phone book from another area that you call frequently. I live near San Francisco and have a San Francisco telephone directory in addition to one for our area. Just call your service representative to request extra books. Verify that there is no charge for obtaining an extra directory.

- Avoid extra call backs. Keep a calendar, paper, and pencils by the telephone so you can jot down important information. Then you won't have to make extra calls to verify information.

- Do not permit the telephone company to make money by selling your name. The telephone company sells a cross-index to businesses, which lists customers by address and by telephone number. A carpet cleaner, say, who wants to sell his service by telephone can use the cross-index to look up your street name and then call everyone on your block. And what a handy guide for burglars! They spot a house, look it up in the cross-index by address, and call to verify that the house is unoccupied. Request by telephone that your address be omitted from future printings of the telephone directory and the cross-index. Your listing should appear:

Your name . . . . . . . . . . . .555-4567

There is no charge to have your address omitted from the directory. You will receive fewer sales calls when your address is not included. Call tomorrow and instruct your service representative to remove your address from the directory and to omit your name, address, and number from cross-indexes.

# Calls

Resist the urge to pick up the phone. Jot down a note or postcard instead of making that toll or long-distance call.

Find out the best time of day to call relatives and friends whom you call frequently, and coordinate with times when rates are lowest. Then you can arrange with the other party to make your phone calls at a certain day and time, so you can count on catching him at home.

Call the telephone company to find out when rates are lowest for making long-distance calls. Rates go down markedly during certain hours.

Gather information about private, discount long-distance telephone services. Most such services connect up only to big cities, but if that's where you do your calling, long distance, discount service may be just the thing for you.

You need a touch-tone phone for this service. If you buy your own phone, make certain it is an electronic push-button phone. Some push-button phones are really rotary phones inside, with buttons on the outside. Touch-tone phones have a registration number ending with a T, rotary phones (with or without buttons) have a registration number ending with an R. You pay a monthly fee. Find out if service is available in the zones where you call and figure out if such service will save you money. If you call frequently, it can save you quite a bit.

Set a timer when you make a long-distance call so you don't chat too long.

Direct-dial to get the lowest rate. Instructions for direct dialing are printed in your telephone directory.

Stop paying for phone calls with bad connections. Hang up and notify the operator *immediately* that you had a poor connection on a long-distance call. The charge for that call will then be eliminated. If you stay on the phone for more than a minute, you will be charged for the call. Then, re-place the call.

# ELECTRICITY AND FUEL

Take steps to reduce the cost of energy. Some ideas are free and others come at a cost. They all result in a saving of money. You can gather information for free. If an insulation company tells you that you can "probably cut your heating bills in half by having your walls insulated," do not take the salesperson's word for it. Call your local utility company and find out exactly how much you will save, considering current energy costs. The insulation company is trying to make a sale and may say almost anything to do so. Verify the information by getting free facts from your utility company who is not trying to sell.

## Energy in general

- Gather information, write or telephone for free information on how you can reduce energy costs in your climate zone. Ask for a list of free publications and free services that may be available for customers.

  Call your local utility company. Get the address and/or phone number from billing information or the phone directory.

  Utilization and Inquiries, Room 507A
  Office of Government and Public Affairs
  United States Department of Agriculture
  Washington, DC 20250. Write for "Agricultural Fact Sheets"

  United States Department of Energy
  Washington, DC 20585

  Consumer Information Center
  Pueblo, Colorado 81009

- Read the information flyers enclosed with your monthly bills. They often list new publications and services to help you save.
- Start a file of booklets, articles, and news clippings on reducing energy costs. Reread them on occasion to make certain you are doing everything possible to keep costs down.

- Borrow books from the public library on saving money and conserving energy. New publications are popping up daily on energy-saving tips for homeowners.
- Cooperate with your utility company by adhering to requests to limit usage during peak hours of the day. When everyone cooperates, everyone saves. In our areas, customers are asked not to use dishwashers, dryers, and washers during the peak energy-consumption hours of noon to 6 P.M.
- Inform family members how much you are paying for monthly heating (or cooling) of your home and for hot water. Then they will understand why you want them to take shorter showers or to close the front door.
- Find out if your utility company will make a house call to analyze your energy needs. We had a free energy audit of our home by the utility company and got valuable advice on how to save money. They can advise you of steps you can take to reduce bills and can tell you exactly how much you will save on current energy costs.

## Heating

- Caulk and weatherstrip those leaky doors and windows. Get how-to books from the library and save money by doing it yourself. Or have screen and storm windows installed. This is one of those pay-now-save-later investments, expensive but worth it in the long run.
- Add insulation to attic, floors, and/or walls according to the requirements for the climate zone in which you live. Your utility company can give you free information on the most effective type and amount of insulation for your house. If you plan to have the work done by a licensed contractor, ask the utility company for a list of recommended contractors.
- Keep furnace filters clean.
- Turn off furnace pilot light in summer. Call your utility company for instructions on doing this. Ask if they will do it for you in late spring and turn it on again when the weather turns cool in the fall.
- Lower your thermostat to 60 or 65 degrees during the day and to 50

or 55 degrees at night. Wear thermal underwear and a sweater indoors if it is chilly.

- Put a clock timer on your thermostat so the heat can click on in the morning just before you rise. Your clock timer can also turn the heat down during the day if everyone is gone. You save money every hour the furnace is turned down or turned off. Warning: In subfreezing temperatures, your pipes may freeze if the temperature is turned off completely.
- Landscaping can reduce fuel costs as well as add to the finished look of your house. Plant evergreen trees and shrubs close to the house walls. Evergreens will insulate the walls from cold winter wind and hot summer air. For maximum effectiveness, shrubs must be planted close together to form a barrier.
- Trees can serve as windbreaks and protect your home from harsh winter winds. Many people like to buy live Christmas trees every year and after the holiday plant them, forming an add-a-tree hedge.
- Shade your house in summer with tall, leafy trees. The shade will result in a cooler house. Choose deciduous trees, so that in winter the sun can shine through the bare boughs.
- Send for a list of "Fact Sheets in Home Weatherization" from Special Programs Center, Office of Government and Public Affairs, United States Department of Agriculture, Washington, D.C. 20250.

# Lights

- Turn off lights not being used and use lower-watt bulbs wherever possible. You may need bright lights in the bathroom for putting on makeup and beside reading chairs, but hallways and stairs can be adequately lighted with lower-wattage bulbs.
- Stop using decorative lighting outside your home.
- Install fluorescent lights wherever possible. They cost less to operate.
- Install dimmer switches so you can adjust lighting according to your needs.

# Water and water heating

- Call your local water company for information on how to conserve water and save on water-heating expenses. Find out if they have water-conservation devices available for free or for sale. Our water company supplies water-conservation kits to customers for free. Availability of the free conservation kits was announced on a flyer with the bill.
- Put a timer in the bathroom for three-minute showers.
- Lower the temperature of your hot water heater. For most households, 100 degrees to 120 degrees is hot enough. If nobody is home during the day, shut it off for those hours.
- Do only full loads of dishes and laundry to conserve water and electricity.
- Turn off your water heater when you go away for a weekend or a vacation. Or put it on the "low" or "vacation" setting.
- Start using warm water instead of hot for white laundry. Wash colored laundry in warm water and rinse everything in cold water. Or wash it all in cold. You will be astonished to see how little difference it makes in how clean your clothes come out looking.
- Set a timer when you turn on outdoor sprinklers so you remember to turn them off. Excessive watering can flood the lawn or garden.
- Put a flow restrictor in your shower head and faucets. You will use far less water.
- Insulate your hot-water tank. Kits are reasonably priced and are easy to install. They quickly pay for themselves from savings on water-heating costs.
- Insulate hot-water pipes with insulating tape. This is another easy, do-it-yourself task that saves money.
- Drip, drip, drip—fix those leaky faucets and toilets. They are costing you money with every single drop.
- Buy an inexpensive children's wading pool for children's summer play instead of permitting them to play for hours with the garden hose. The sun will warm the pool water. Set it up in different spots so you can water the lawn when you dump the pool. Warning: *Keep close watch on young children when playing in or near water.*

- Water should be 140 degrees or hotter to make dishes get really clean in your automatic dishwasher. When you buy a dishwasher, get one that has a heating unit just for the dishwasher. Then you can set the water heater temperature at 120 degrees or lower. To save on electricity for drying dishes in your automatic dishwasher, turn off the dishwasher when it reaches the dry cycle. My dishwasher takes about forty minutes to reach the dry cycle. I set a timer for forty minutes when I start up the dishwasher.
- Check Energyguide ratings (yellow and black stickers on appliances) when making purchases. An appliance with a better energy rating may cost you more, but you will save that money and more through lower operating costs. Ask for an explanation of the Energyguide labels if you are not sure how to interpret them.
- Make a list of what is in the freezer and mark packages clearly. Then you won't waste time and energy searching for something that isn't there.
- Place items in a particular location so they can be located quickly. I put juice and all snack items in one area in the refrigerator. My kids can quickly grab what they want and close the door.

## Clothes dryer

- Try to use your dryer as little as possible. It's a big gobbler of electricity. Hang clothes on plastic hangers to dry outdoors, on shower rod, or in a doorway.
- Tumble slow-to-dry garments like blue jeans and towels until they are half-dry. Then hang them on hangers to finish drying overnight.
- Keep the lint filter clean. Your dryer takes much longer to dry clothing when the lint filter is clogged.
- Don't overdry clothes. It causes excessive wrinkling and costs money.
- Fold clothing immediately to reduce or eliminate ironing.
- If you have a room that gets warm from the heater, string up a clothesline for fast indoor drying.
- Buy a wooden drying rack and put it in the bathtub for out-of-the-way indoor drying.

- Go solar—the sunshine is free. Put up a washline and hang laundry out of doors. An empty plastic hanging-flower container makes a great clothespin holder.

# Appliance buying

- Check consumer publications to get the most value for your dollar.
- Survey relatives and friends to find out which brands they have found to be most reliable. Or most unreliable.
- Decide on the model and brand you want and then price-shop by telephone. Negotiate the price. When I bought my washer and dryer, the salesperson said there would be a $25 delivery charge. I told them I could not afford to pay for the delivery and would have to shop elsewhere. The fee was promptly waived. The store wants your business, so be tough. Get the best price you can. You can also try to get a discount for buying with cash. With a cash sale, the store saves the percentage it has to pay the credit-card companies. It never hurts to ask.
- You can count on energy costs to continue to escalate. Read the Energyguide yellow and black stickers, and buy accordingly.
- Avoid buying the top-of-the-line, gimmick-laden appliance model. More buttons, cycles, and flashing lights usually means more repair problems. My rule of thumb is to buy the middle-of-the-line model instead of either the stripped-down economy model or the "Cadillac." That way, I get the devices I need and will use.
- Stick with the brands that have given you good service. After fourteen years of using one kind of washer and dryer, I was so pleased with its quality that I bought another set of the same durable brand. Together the two sets stood the test of four children and more laundry than I want to think about, with very few service calls. Sometimes the best models cost more initially but repay you by rarely needing repair. Check the Consumer's Union *Buying Guide*.

- Resist advertising hype that makes you want appliances you can easily manage without. No, thanks—I don't need an electric potato peeler, no matter how happy that lady looks in the magazine ad. I don't need hot-doggers and bacon-cookers and hamburger-patty flatteners (what's wrong with the human hand?) and other devices that take up room and are too unversatile to do more than one job.
- Teach your family how to use your appliances properly. I posted a sign above the washer with an arrow pointing which way to turn the dial. This avoids breakage and costly service calls.
- Install an on/off switch on the cord of your "instant-on" television. "Instant on" sets drain power constantly—when turned "off."
- Avoid purchasing appliances that keep on costing you money:
  coffeepots that require paper filters
  vacuum cleaners with disposable paper bags
  trash compactors, which use energy and require liner bags and deodorant spray
- Save directions, warranties, and saleslips. Put all guarantee information in a file box or envelope. Take a few moments to staple the sales slip to the warranty. Then you have a record of when you purchased the item, how much you paid, and where you bought it, and you can return it without a hassle. Many stores have a "no returns without sales slip policy." When something breaks, check the guarantee—you may be entitled to a free replacement or repair. Much to my amazement, my typewriter had a five-year warranty on all parts. It paid off to keep that sales slip. When I took it in to be repaired, all parts were free. To be an assertive expert at making returns to stores see page 147.
- Keep a record on major appliances you purchase. I use a section of my recipe box. I jot on a 3 × 5″ card the model number, date of purchase, cost, and date when warranty expires. If I have a service call, I jot it on the card. I note the reason for the call and the cost of service. Then when I need to replace a major appliance, I can look at the card to see how much service cost over the years. That will help me decide if I want to buy that brand again.

*Maytag Washer*     *bought May 1, 1978*
*Model EL14*       *Warranty x May 1, 1979*

*Cost $422.—*      *Gemco, Cupertino Store*

*Service:*

# Reduce your trash

Recycle aluminum cans, glass, and newspapers to make less trash for you and the Planet Earth.
- Newspapers can be rolled up into newspaper logs to burn in the fireplace. Just roll them up by hand (you don't need that special roller device) and fasten with wire. Cardboard is also an excellent kindling. Instead of discarding boxes, cut them up, save them, and pile them around the logs when you want to start a fire.
- Buy soft drinks only in all-aluminum recyclable cans (check the can—it will carry a label if it's the right kind), for those with steel tops cannot be used again. If your favorite soda pop comes in steel-top-cans, buy it in bottles instead and find an agency nearby that recycles bottles.

# 10

# GREAT GIFTS

Giving the right present to a friend or family member is a very satisfying experience. And the good part is that Great Gifts do not have to break your budget. With just a bit of care and planning, you can give ideal gifts every time. If you start with a list of people you buy gifts for and write down their sizes as well as their special interests, you'll be armed with the information you need to launch yourself in truly creative gift buying. Keep an eye out for good buys whenever you shop, and when you find something that seems just right, buy it. Store your goodies in a box or carton in an out-of-the-way closet or shelf. Just knowing they're there will make you feel good.

One important fact to remember is that it's difficult to shop wisely when you are pressed for time. So try to avoid those frantic last-minute gift-buying expeditions. When you know you have to buy something *or else,* you tend to spend more than you should and often choose things that aren't quite right. By shopping in advance you avoid this problem. Also, do start taking advantage of postholiday sales. Buy marked-down specialities to add to your collection. Heart-shaped soaps that you buy for half price after Valentine's Day are appealing presents all year long.

The fun part of having a bagful of gifts tucked away is that you can treat *yourself* to a delightful little gift every now and then. Go on—you deserve it.

## GREAT GIFTS LISTS

Probably the best way to keep the cost of gift-giving within realistic limits is to combine two or three reasonably priced items into one ideal present. Read over the list of Great Gifts suggested below and use it as a starting place to put together terrific-to-give and fun-to-get combinations. Of course, some of these gifts are great all by themselves.

Gift items that cost less than $5 are listed first. Suggestions are provided so you can add related items to increase the value of the gift. You can spend as little or as much as you wish. It's fun to group together several items into an interesting gift. Gift ideas are listed under gifts for children, for adults, and for everyone. As you read the lists, other ideas will pop into your head. Jot down your ideas at the end of each list. Star or underline items on the list that you especially like. Write names of family and friends to whom you might give certain gifts. Take advantage of sales and start buying and tucking away your very special collection of Great Gifts.

# Great gifts for children under $5

| GIFTS | RELATED ITEMS—BUY ONE OR MORE |
| --- | --- |
| easy-to-grow seed packets or seedlings for flowers or vegetables | hand towel, sprinkling can |
| how-to-draw books (animals, cartoons, castles, etc.) | sketch tablet, art pencil, felt pens |
| small-chalkboard and chalk (for playing school) | red pencils, pencil sharpener, crayons, stick-on stars |
| educational materials; send for free catalog;<br>Frank Schaffer Publ. Inc., Dept. BJ<br>1028 Via Mirabel<br>Palos Verdes Estates, California 90274 | same as above |
| bank | 100 pennies |
| art paper | felt pens, crayons, scissors |
| picture frame (for photo or child's artwork) | |
| tape or record | ear plug or pillow speaker |
| ceramic mug | packets of hot chocolate |
| map of city or state where they live | magnifying glass |
| book on shell or rock collecting | magnifying glass, some shell or rock specimens |
| photo album | roll of film |
| scrapbook for collecting schoolwork, art, birthday cards etc. | special stickers to decorate scrapbook |
| flashlight | extra batteries |
| toolbox | hammer, screwdriver, nails, measuring tape |
| wall map of world or U.S. | stamps of state flags |

| GIFTS | RELATED ITEMS—BUY ONE OR MORE |
|---|---|
| child's cookbook | apron, potholders |
| stamp album | packet of stamps for collectors |
| address book with names and addresses of family and friends | postcards, writing paper, and stamps |
| houseplant | plant food, watering can, mister |
| decks of cards and dice | |
| magnets | |
| novelty pillowcase with favorite character or cartoon decoration | |
| blank cassette tapes | |
| movie pass | |
| nylon pup tent from surplus store | |
| nylon duffel bag | |
| magazine subscription to fit special interest | |
| canvas tote bag or book bag | |
| key chain | |
| kaleidoscope | |

## Great gifts for adults under $5

| | |
|---|---|
| sun visor | sun-block lotion |
| camera strap | film, camera bag, camera-cleaning kit |
| plant for house or yard | plant food, plant-care book |
| clay flower pots and seed packets for herbs or flowers | gardening gloves, trowel, plant food |
| ceramic mug | herbal teas, special coffee, and tea ball |

| GIFTS | RELATED ITEMS—BUY ONE OR MORE |
|-------|-------------------------------|
| foam-plastic picnic ice chest | paper plates, cups, plastic utensils, paper napkins |
| bread cookbook | breadboard and knife, bread-baking pans |
| cookie cookbook | cookie sheet |
| speciality (soup, seafood, stews) cookbook | apron, potholders, unusual spices |
| book on parenting for expectant parents | baby rattle, pacifier, baby thermometer |
| do-it-yourself home-repair book | screwdriver (Phillips or regular), Band-Aids |
| herbs chart or book | seed packets or seedlings of herbs to grow |
| bottle of wine | cork puller, wine book, wineglasses |
| how-to-take-better-pictures book | roll of film, photo album, camera strap |
| cocktail napkins and hors d'ouevres toothpicks | book on mixing drinks |
| notepaper or stationery | felt pens for writing in kicky colors |
| suntan lotion and stamps for postcards (for a person going on trip) | deck of cards, fat paperback book, good map |
| decks of cards | book to improve your bridge game, bridge tallies |
| fancy soaps | pretty paper guest towels |
| fireplace matches | artificial fireplace log (or a real one) |
| extra-long phone cord | shoulder rest for phone, new telephone-address book |
| recipe box with cards and dividers | include your favorite recipe and nonperishable ingredients needed for preparation |

| GIFTS | RELATED ITEMS—BUY ONE OR MORE |
|---|---|
| plastic tote tray | fill with garden tools<br>fill with cleaning products |
| Chinese cookbook | 5-spice powder for Chinese cookery, implements for wok cooking |
| Italian cookbook | wood or plastic spaghetti lifter |
| all-purpose basket | fill with fruit—one of each—or a busy green plant |
| six-pack of beer<br>Make six fun beer-sampling gifts; Buy six six-packs of six different, unusual beers. Divide the beer so each six-pack contains the bottle or can of each kind. | pretzels, peanuts |

## More Great Gifts

Prepare a survival kit. Spend from just a few dollars on up—it depends how many goodies you pop into the survival kit. Put the kit in a bag, box, or plastic dishpan (see gift bags p. 191).

- **Survival kit for student living away from home for first time:** Band-Aids, aspirin, scotch tape, glue, pen, pencils, tiny pencil sharpener, stamps, envelopes, tablet, stapler, staples, ruler, sewing kit, screwdriver, hammer, paperback dictionary, shoelaces, etc.
- **Survival kit for new car owner:** maps, visor mirror, key ring, flares, no-spill traveling mug, car record book, dimes for phone calls to keep in glove compartment, jumper cables, ice scraper, car-wash solution, sponge, squeegie for windows, nozzle for motor-oil can, large-size funnel, plastic suction hose, etc.
- **Survival kit for traveler:** sewing kit, aspirin, upset-stomach or

diarrhea remedy, stamps, pen, sunscreen, toothpaste, hand lotion, moist towelettes, shampoo, etc.

- **Survival kit for new parents:** tote bag containing baby powder, baby lotion, disposable diapers, pacifier, rattle, moist towelettes, etc.
- **Survival kit for the office worker:** instant coffee pot or immersion heater, coffee, tea, hot chocolate, instant soup, box of crackers, Band-Aids, shoelaces, nail file, etc.
- **Survival kit for pet owner:** book on pet care, leash, pet treats, pet shampoo, pet ID tag, pet toys, etc.
- **Survival kit for flea market/garage sale addict:** heavy canvas tote bag, tape measure, magnifying glass, memo pad, city map.

# Great gifts for everyone under $5

| GIFTS | RELATED ITEMS—BUY ONE OR MORE |
|---|---|
| picture frame | include enlarged photo |
| photo album | include photos or roll of film |
| outdoor thermometer | |
| bird feeder | bag of bird seed or bird-watching guide |
| rain gauge | |
| calendar with important dates and events marked | |
| puzzles and board games | |
| memo pads in different shapes, colors, and sizes | felt pens in kicky colors |
| glass storage jar | filled with nuts, gum drops, etc. |
| magazine subscription | |
| book on nearby city | |

# TOYS FOR CHILDREN

Some toys become favorites and others just sit on the shelf. What makes the difference? The difference is that some toys are interesting because they can be used in many ways. Others quickly become boring because they have only one use. For example, a wind-up toy duck that waddles and says "Quack, quack," gets uninteresting rather fast. A set of building blocks can be used to build houses, forts, castles, highways, and can be used in conjunction with other toys; it will have sustained interest while the wind-up duck is collecting dust.

## Consider this list of ideas when you shop for toys for children

- Inspect toys for workmanship. If you are buying something for a toddler, make certain there are no sharp edges and no swallowing-size pieces.
- If the child attends preschool, find out if you can purchase toys and playthings through the child's school. Preschools may have catalogs showing toys that parents do not find in toy stores. We bought wood blocks through our parent cooperative nursery school. Of all the toys we bought for our children, blocks were the most frequently used. My kids used them throughout elementary school, and when playmates came over, the blocks were virtually always used.
- Buy games you can play with your child. I think the old-fashioned, non-electronic board games are the best. My kids still play Monopoly, Sorry, and Scrabble.
- The more the toy is active, and a child has to watch it, instead of participating, the less interesting the toy is. Sitting and watching gets quickly boring. Active involvement generates interest and correlates with learning.
- Talk to your children about toys that are advertised on television. If the plane doesn't really fly, explain that to your child: Point out that the commercial is designed to make it look like it flies. You can help

your child become more sophisticated about advertising hype by discussing overglamourized products sold on television.

- Don't hesitate to buy a tea set or a baby carriage for a boy and trucks and trains for girls. When our son Steve was three, he loved to play with water. I bought him an aluminum tea set and a plastic dishpan and he washed his dishes daily in the backyard. Our son Michael begged for a baby carriage for his birthday like his playmate had. We bought him one, much to the horror of several fathers in the neighborhood. He had a grand time racing baby carriages up and down the sidewalk with his friend. He also filled it with water, trucks, dirt, you name it. It was one of his favorite toys. Our youngest boy loved the housekeeping corner and the dressups in nursery school. Boys and girls like to play with the same things. Let them explore all sorts of activities and toys rather than thinking of some toys as being exclusively for one sex.
- As a general rule, buy brand name toys. Brand name toys have been tested for safety and are usually worth the extra cost.
- If you are buying a toy as a gift, telephone the child's parent and ask if the toy is suitable if you are unsure.
- Don't forget about records, tapes and books. A book is my favorite gift for a child.
- When you're thinking of buying a gift for a child, look over playthings and toys which I've gleaned from my experiences as a parent and elementary teacher:
    sand
    blocks
    baby dolls (plain, no batteries or gimmicks)
    trucks small enough to be held in child's hand
    medium and large trucks
    doll house
    Fisher-Price "little people" stuff: firehouse, airport, farm, . . .
    Lego buildsets
    board games
    wooden snap trains
    puzzles
    old clothing for dress ups

tea sets (non-breakable)
scrap wood, hammer and nails (for appropriate age child)
kits to build models
kits to make leathergoods
loom to weave potholders
books
records
art materials—paper, felt pens, scissors

## GIFTS YOU MAKE YOURSELF

Homemade presents can be the most appreciated gifts of all. Here are some ideas for free or low-cost gifts to delight your family and friends. Check out books from the public library on simple gifts to make. Photocopy the ideas you like. Start a file of "gifts to make" from ideas you see in newspapers and magazines. The November and December issues are loaded with instructions and ideas for free or low-cost homemade gifts. Here are some more from me.

# Food and drink

- Treasured recipes are wonderful gifts to give and receive, usually for novice cooks. Copy some of your favorite recipes on recipe cards. Put them in a plastic file box for a perfect, much appreciated gift for a bridal shower. Or combine with jars of herbs and spices. If it's a recipe for cake or cookies, include a sample.
- Compile a "family heirloom" cookbook. Ask, or write to, relatives for as many of their favorite recipes as possible, and combine them into a cookbook of treasured family dishes. Print or type the recipes and make as many photocopies as the number of family cookbooks you want. You might paste photocopied recipes onto recipe cards and fasten them with a binder ring or paste them into a blank booklet. Be sure to put everyone's name beside the recipe she contributed.

- Make up a batch of your specialty, bottle or can it, and pass it around. Here is the recipe for my special coffee liqueur, which has made a big hit with the recipients on my gift lists.

    *Coffee Liqueur* (makes 1 gallon)

    1 four-ounce jar instant coffee

    7 cups sugar

    4 cups water, heated to boiling

    ½ gallon vodka (cheapest you can find)

    2 whole vanilla beans

        or

    2 tablespoons vanilla extract (cheaper than beans)

Mix instant coffee, sugar, and boiling water. Stir until coffee and sugar are dissolved and let stand until cool. Set aside for several hours. Add vodka. Cut vanilla beans open lengthwise and cut each half in two. Pour coffee-vodka mixture into a gallon glass bottle (or two half-gallon bottles). Add vanilla bean (or extract) and cap tightly. Let stand for 30 days. Every 5 days, gently shake bottle to mix. After the 30 days are up, decant into smaller bottles, discarding vanilla bean. (I use clean beer bottles with twist-off caps.)

You may want to give friends suggestions on some ways to enjoy their specially brewed coffee liqueur.

Drink it.

Add 1 ounce to hot coffee plus a dollop of whipped cream.

Add 1 ounce to a cup of eggnog (my favorite).

Add 2 ounces of vodka to 1 ounce of coffee liqueur to make a Black Russian cocktail.

Pour 2 ounces over vanilla ice cream.

You can mix up a gallon of this delicious liqueur for very little money compared to the commercial kind. Not only does it cost less, but it tastes far better.

# Nature's bounty

- Gather pine cones and other appealing dried materials (acorns, small branches, seed pods) as a special gift for urban friends or people who might not get to the woods. Put them into a clear plastic bag and tie them with a bright red ribbon.

- If you have nut trees, give a bagful of nuts to be used in holiday cookies and cakes. Or shell them and give a jarful of ready-to-eat goodies.
- If you have a green thumb, make cuttings of your favorite house-plants to show your friends you care. Buy a bunch of red clay flowerpots. Then make the cuttings and start them in a jar of water on a sunny windowsill. Watch the roots grow and then plant them in planter mix in one of the clay pots. Before you know it, you'll have a batch of bushy plants. Give them (with a card telling how to care for them) to lucky friends.
- We give our friends and neighbors a "Yule Log" every holiday season. It is a split log decorated with greens, small pine cones, and a few berries if possible. (I do this project in the basement or garage and place the logs on newspapers. Then wax dribbles won't damage anything. I use a hand trowel to scoop out the hot wax.) Melt some paraffin wax in an empty coffee can over a low flame. Put a mound of soft wax on each log and press greens into the wax. The wax will hold the greens in place when it hardens. Add a red bow, and deliver the "Yule Log." Friends tell us that burning the log has become a part of their holiday tradition.

# Magic moisturizer

Magic Cream is a marvelous face cream you can concoct in minutes in the kitchen. Use it as a night cream for your face, on rough heels and elbows, or to remove eye makeup. Everyone in our family uses it—men included. Give little jars of Magic Cream to friends as gifts—they'll love it.

### MAGIC CREAM

3 tablespoons lanolin (buy from the pharmacist at drug counter)
3 tablespoons olive oil (from grocery store)
2 tablespoons commercial moisturizer skin cream (use an inexpensive brand of face cream)

Melt lanolin in the olive oil over low heat. Stir in commercial moisturizing cream and remove from heat. Pour in a jar and cool, stirring occasionally. I use an empty face-cream jar to hold Magic Cream.

# Gift

Colorful booklets of coupons you make yourself for free services are terrific no-cost gifts. The recipient can "cash in" these coupons whenever he wants. Be creative and add your ideas to the following list of services:

cut the grass
run an errand
take you to a movie
make a German chocolate cake (or whatever your specialty)
give a back rub
do a flower arrangement
babysit
walk the dog
bathe the dog
wash the windows
clean the car inside and out
clean the garage
serve breakfast in bed

# Sew simple

- Stitch gifts with your sewing machine. Quick-to-stitch gifts are fun to make—look in the pattern books for ideas. Tote bags from quilted, washable fabric in a cheery print are super gifts. Patterns are available in the pattern books. Friends will love them for carting around sewing projects, taking along books or magazines on a trip, or carting stuff to the beach. Quilted tote bags can be tossed in washer and dryer when necessary.
- Tablecloth and napkin sets you make to match a friend's kitchen are an attractive, personalized gift. Use no-iron fabric for easy care.

For a long, rectangular table, make an elegant table runner instead of a tablecloth.

• Make bright holiday gift bags. Buy striped, printed, or plain fabric and sew a bunch of gift bags. The person who receives the gift can reuse the gift bag. In our own household, I save gift bags and reuse them after a family member has opened a gift. Fabric is available at Christmastime in cute, holiday prints—buy it at 50 percent off the day after Christmas. Buy some to make holiday tablecloths and napkin sets, too. Tie the bags with colorful, fluffy yarn and make them in all sizes. The big ones are especially handy for items that take yards of wrapping paper. Make a set of gift bags for yourself and for a friend.

Bag of wine is a terrific hostess, birthday, or housewarming gift. It looks elegant and costs very little. Buy a bottle of wine and stitch up a giftbag to hold it. Include a wine opener in the bag for a super gift everyone can use and enjoy.

## Gift-wrap ideas

Gift wrap can cost as much as the gift itself unless you are a careful shopper. Some money-saving tips for gift-wrappings.

• Pop yourself some packing material. If you have a hot-air popcorn popper you can pop a batch of non-greasy popcorn. If you are wrapping a fragile gift or mailing a fragile object, pack it in popcorn. Works just as well as the plastic packing materials you can buy and it is cheaper. When I sent a package of home-baked goodies packed in popcorn to my son Steve in college, he ate the goodies AND the popcorn!

• Wrap a gift for a child in the color comics from the Sunday newspaper.

• Wrap a kitchen gift in a terry tea towel.

• Use colored tissue paper instead of wrapping paper—it is pretty and cheaper.

• Cut fabric with a pinking shears in one-inch-wide ribbons. Cute print fabrics make attractive "ribbons."

- Buy giant rolls of wrapping paper instead of many shorter rolls. But first read the label to find out the number of yards or square feet you get. The thickness of the roll is determined by the cardboard tube, not the amount of paper you get for your money. Read and compare to get the best buy.
- Order gift-wrap supplies by mail at low cost. Send to Current for a free catalog of marvelous gift items and wrapping supplies. Their prices go down when you order more than a certain number of items. Get together a group order with friends, neighbors, or co-workers.

  Current, Inc.
  The Current Building
  Colorado Springs, CO 80941

# HOLIDAY GIFT GIVING

Holiday shopping can demolish your budget and sap your strength. It does not have to be that way. Shop smart all year round and you will save yourself time and money at holiday time. Best of all, you'll be able to sit back and enjoy the season.

- Shopping cards make picking up unexpected bargains more likely. For each family member, carry a $3 \times 5''$ index card (with sizes and color preferences). When you see something great at a sale, you'll be ready to buy it. Mark that purchase on the card. This prevents duplication. (I've recommended this for clothes shopping for your family but it also works well for all sorts of gifts, so I thought it worth repeating here).
- Start your Christmas shopping in January. On your brand-new calendar, jot down items you will need for next holiday season. Put these items in appropriate months, for example, wrapping paper, ribbon and gift tags should be noted down in October or November, so you have plenty of time to order by mail or get a jump on the season.

- If gift-giving has gotten out of hand in your family—with expectations sometimes reaching a level suitable for a Texas oil king and his family, it may be time to consider changing your gift-giving customs. In some families with older kids this problem has been solved by having every family member draw one name. Then instead of Mom and Dad being Mr. & Mrs. Santa Claus, everyone shares the shopping and expenses.

  Another alternative is to treat the family to one big gift everyone will enjoy. It could be a special trip or a new tape deck.

- Taper off your gift buying. Many people exchange gifts with far-away relatives because they have always done it. Each year it becomes more difficult to select a gift for someone you rarely see. If you have people on your gift-exchange list for whom you really do not want to buy gifts, send them a note well before the time the gift is due. Suggest that this year you send a token food gift and then both discontinue buying gifts. The feeling is probably mutual, and your suggestion will be met with a sigh of relief. In our family, the idea of stopping our long-distance gift giving was welcome and was received without hurt feelings.

- Give yourself the gift of fun. If you have a relative or friend who gives you money to spend, why not treat yourself to a special experience instead of buying a gift? Taking the family to a show or going out for a special lunch or dinner can be more fun than having another package to unwrap. Take a snapshot of the family entering the amusement park and send it with a note to the person who gave you the money to spend for the family. He will probably be delighted to see that you had a fun experience with his gift of money.

# Share your tips for making and saving money with Barbara Jean

Write: BARBARA JEAN
      Box 2722
      Saratoga, California 95070

Send me your original ideas for saving and making money. If your ideas are used in forthcoming hint books by me, you will be notified and sent an autographed copy of my next book. Submission of an idea constitutes permission for it to be published in any forthcoming book by Barbara Jean.

I'm looking forward to hearing from you.

*Barbara Jean*

# INDEX